TREAT
yourself

**70 Classic Snacks You Loved
as a Kid (*and Still Love Today*)**

Jennifer Steinhauer

PHOTOGRAPHS BY JAMES RANSOM

CLARKSON POTTER/PUBLISHERS
New York

Copyright © 2014 by Jennifer Steinhauer
Photographs copyright © 2014 by James Ransom

All rights reserved.
Published in the United States by Clarkson Potter/Publishers, an
imprint of the Crown Publishing Group, a division of Random House
LLC, a Penguin Random House Company, New York.
www.crownpublishing.com
www.clarksonpotter.com

CLARKSON POTTER is a trademark and POTTER with colophon is a
registered trademark of Random House LLC.

Library of Congress Cataloging-in-Publication Data
Steinhauer, Jennifer.
   Treat yourself : 70 classic snacks you loved as a kid
(and still love today) / Jennifer Steinhauer ; photographs
by James Ransom. — First edition.
      p. cm
   Includes index.
1. Desserts. 2. Snack foods. I. Title.
   TX773.S838 2014
   641.86—dc23   2013032509

ISBN 978-0-385-34520-0
eBook ISBN 978-0-385-34521-7

Printed in China

Book and cover design by Rae Ann Spitzenberger
Cover photographs by James Ransom

10 9 8 7 6 5 4 3 2 1

First Edition

TO HANNAH
AND SADIE,
WHO REDEFINE
DELICIOUS FOR
ME EVERY DAY.

CONTENTS

INTRODUCTION

For Americans of a certain age, memory lane is paved with Ho Hos. This coiled snack cake was my gateway commercial confection in the 1970s, tucked into my lunch next to a wax paper–wrapped peanut butter and grape jelly sandwich and some immediately discarded green grapes.

I would eat my Ho Hos with some slightly warm milk, courtesy of the unsmiling lunch lady, whom I would run into later in life in an unsavory darts bar in my hometown of Kalamazoo, Michigan. Sometimes I traded my Ho Hos for Ding Dongs, the hockey puck–shaped treats that struck me as an acceptable alternative to my workingman's tiny *bûche de Noël.*

I moved on to Twinkies, purchased by my dad at the 7-Eleven with a *Mad* magazine (mine) and a pack of Merit Lights (his). I sat in the car, listening to Olivia Newton-John on the radio, singing along and waiting for him to return and toss me my bounty. As we

OPPOSITE: The love of a chip starts young. Me, at Loy Norrix High School (Kalamazoo, Michigan), 1986.

made our way down Kilgore Road, the car would slowly fill with a cloud of smoke as I pulled at the cellophane wrapper and began to flip through my magazine, absentmindedly singing along to Olivia.

The Twinkie was later followed by the Suzy Q, a monstrosity of cream-stuffed devil's food cake that was forever tainted after Dad used one to conceal a giant bolus of penicillin. By high school, I was a junk food connoisseur, carefully putting together midday meals curated largely by Hostess. In between the scarfed snack cakes, there were plenty of other confections, of course: Oreos eaten sandwich cream first; Thin Mints that we waited for all year, sold door-to-door and by actual Girl Scouts (not by parents at the office, as is so often the case these days); chocolate-covered marshmallows that my mother hid for herself. And Windmill cookies. But who really liked those? Well, Dad did.

If there was even the seed of a notion in my parents' heads that chemically stabilized, highly caloric snack foods were perhaps a suboptimal regular addition to our diets, it was never expressed. But a midwestern childhood in the 1980s was largely absent parental dietary laws. When in grade school, we rode our bikes wherever we wanted until the sun began to fade and it seemed wise to get home, or until someone fell and needed a Band-Aid. After school, we watched *Guiding Light* or *The Brady Bunch* and then mulled over doing homework that no parent would review. We ate Honey Buns at will.

I grew up, and Twinkies slowly disappeared from my life, along with sloe gin and takeout hamburgers and French fries dipped in mayonnaise. Adults did not, in my view, lick the center out of a cupcake in public. Still, my passions remained under the surface, a fire I could not put out!

When I learned that Hostess had filed for bankruptcy protection, signaling the potential demise of my former lunchtime treats, I began to wonder if I could emulate Hostess snack cakes, as well as a variety of other much-loved junk food from my past—from Twinkies to Honey Buns to Fritos to Junior Mints—right in my own kitchen. I began with the classic Twinkie, and I purchased the truly extraneous baking closet item, the canoe pan, which conveniently comes with a handy cream injector. I was stunned and tickled to realize it was possible to re-create this snack treat almost to perfection with very few steps.

The next project was the cupcakes, Hostess's most popular snack cake, one that finds its chocolate base in cocoa and ends with a boiled chocolate ganache that, once cooled and applied, will not quite peel back like plastic, as does the original, but will rather slither onto the tongue in a bittersweet jig. I also tried my hand at homemade Oreos, as well as another childhood favorite, Fritos, which my husband, who is from Texas, spent his childhood eating in their most delightful form: in the bag with chili poured on top—the Frito pie, preferably eaten in the stands at a Little League game.

I would chronicle this culinary adventure in the *New York Times*, where I have been a reporter for almost two decades, and was astounded by reader response, both in the elegiac musings about snack foods past and in the surprising enthusiasm for making such treats at home. I suspect much of the avidity stemmed from the general nostalgia sparked by foods from our youth and from a bit of regional pride. The sug-

Hostess Cup Cakes
p. 90

ary film of fruit pie frosting transports me to my friend Carolyn's house, where I would chow down while doing geometry homework and catching peeks at her hot older brother, who was recently, and excitingly in my view, expelled from school. I would learn from readers about the potato chips that made track meets bearable, the candy bars eaten only at the movies, the Funyuns that were devoured only at a boyfriend's house because they were not permitted at home.

Snack foods, of course, have always given Americans pleasure, or at least since the late nineteenth century, when Cracker Jack got its start; through the 1930s, when potato chips hit the scene; and on through World War II, when commercial packaging advances turned local treats into regional and, eventually, national sensations. Still, specific traditions endured. The South had its MoonPies. The people of Philadelphia alone could claim Tastykakes, and Hydrox cookies were the kosher choice over Oreos at one time. Snack foods are cultural totems that place their consumer in regions and time frames, in memories good and difficult.

I have worked at the *New York Times* my entire journalism career. I began as a copy girl in college, then became a news clerk in a reporting training program, and in 1995 graduated to full-time reporter, eventually covering Capitol Hill. In most of these positions, I often snuck my love of food into my day job, writing regularly for the food section and the *New York Times*

Raisinets
p. 151

Magazine about restaurants, ingredients, food trends, and dining culture.

But nothing prepared me for the response to the homemade snack food exploration.

One reader wrote: "In Mississippi, we had Hoot'n Toots—just like Suzy Q's and Ho Hos, I think. I always thought that snack cake name was hilarious."

Another said: "Anyone from Eastern PA and NJ knows about Butterscotch Krimpets."

Or simply: "What happened to Chocodiles?"

In this era of whole grain goodness, I was surprised to find that Hostess Cup Cakes and their ilk seemed to strike a chord. There seemed to be a craving for someone to share more snack recipes.

Further, there was the realization that while making homemade junk food is both fun and evocative, it is also a bit healthier than eating shelf-stabilized, chemically festooned commercial snack foods, which many of us would no sooner touch—or feed to our families—than plant fertilizer. Today's snackers will be relieved to note that a one-ounce serving of commercial Fritos has twice the calories of the oven-made version in this book, and not necessarily because one is fried and the other baked; it is likely that the commercial version has quite a bit of fat mixed into the dough. Few of these homemade treats have more calories than the originals, and even when they do, they are absent the unpronounceable chemicals and stabilizers of the store-bought versions that many people eschew.

So, with the insatiable craving established, this cookbook came to be. On behalf of those readers who harbor the desire to once again know a Funny Bones, I lugged home a fifty-pound bag of flour from Costco, plowed through thirty-seven pounds of butter and a hundred sheets of parchment paper, and force-fed my colleagues pile upon pile of misshapen vanilla cookies and burned Nutter Butters. My family ate a bit more takeout for dinner, consoled by knowing they would always have something interesting to bring to a volleyball tournament when it was their turn to provide the snacks. Like so many in our "Do as I say, not as I did" culinary generation, I have never actually purchased Twinkies or Ding Dongs for my children, but they took great delight in seeing them made in our kitchen.

Oh, there were some sad times, like one Thanksgiving when, an hour before dinner, my mixer discharged marshmallow fluff onto my kitchen ceiling and most of my cabinetry. I may or may not have screamed at my entire family, "YOU NEVER HELP ME WITH ANYTHING!!!" but I really can't be sure. But overall, re-creating these treats was largely exciting, as memories moved from the mixing bowl to the napkins of delighted friends and coworkers who shared their own childhood memories of illicit nibbling.

Moreover, these treats readily adapt themselves to updating. You can elevate a treat from your memory with contemporary touches: for instance, I feel my life was totally changed by adding sea salt to a recipe for home-baked Lorna Doone shortbread cookies. (Well, in truth, life didn't really change that much, because I still got stuck cleaning the pans. But the cookies were insanely good.)

It's true that the absence of chemicals and big machines that give commercial snacks their uniformity will change the texture, the aesthetics, and sometimes the flavor of your home-made goods. Your cookies won't have those regal patterns that commercial brands sport and may lack a certain snap that only cookies meant to wait on a truck-stop shelf for months have been created to offer. With this cookbook, you will be tempering chocolate and using a number of good ingredients, not adding the bits of oil and cheap stabilizers that food companies often use to get chocolate to behave. It's worth the sacrifice of the "snap" for the deliciousness. Indeed, I found, as the literary types would say, constitutive tension between authenticity and deliciousness—I wanted the snacks to be as I remembered them, but I, and others, always preferred them improved. Over and over again my tasters during this project would coo, "This is so much better than the original!" I loved hearing it, but it also meant that my recipe did not precisely remind them of the treat they ate as kids.

The reason most people haven't tasted these treats in many years is that the experience ends up being disappointing. The truth is, some food memories are anchored in the authentic and the delicious. Your mother's meatloaf, your aunt's arroz con pollo—those foods are both actually delicious and evocative of a time, place, and person that has meaning for you. But other food memories are rounded and softened by the poetry of passed time. You love Hostess fruit pies because they remind you of being on the swim team and eating them before practice, but perhaps if you tasted one now, the artificial flavors and chemicals would sit heavy in your mouth, clouding that memory. Were they really that delicious back then?

The goal here is not only to reproduce those great treats but also to make them better, a crossroads of memory and actual divinity. No one will mistake your Nutter Butters for anything else; they will know just what they are and will like them more than the original. I promise.

In some cases, I make the journey easier—and more authentic—with the use of some store-bought goods. When making fry pies, for instance, frozen dough is your friend, but with Pop-Tarts, you want to make your own dough. While a few of these treats are a bit more complicated or multistepped than others, I have erred whenever possible on the side of ease.

Whatever your favorite junk food memory, my hope is that as you create your homemade treats, it comes back to you with pleasure. I have been surprised at how often I have thought of my father, long gone, and his connection to all that I once ate. He must have been there even when I didn't realize it, nibbling on his Windmill cookie in the dark, as I moved along and on.

Oreos
p. 58

SUPPLIES

In one of my first apartments, I made cookies on disposable baking sheets in an oven held closed with some twine, and I substituted pasta pots when I was too poor for proper mixing bowls. Ask any chef: ingredients and skill trump equipment every time. Still, if you are serious about baking, there are a few minimal supplies that will make life in the kitchen easier.

Bench scraper: A metal bench scraper is essential for cutting dough; it has measurements that can be used to determine the thickness of the dough you're rolling out, and it has a nice sharp edge for slicing. This tool is great for frosting cakes and can be used to scrape crumbs off your work space, too. Bonus: The bench scraper looks vaguely threatening, so it's good to have nearby if someone is trying to sneak a cookie before it's cooled.

Candy thermometer: A candy thermometer is optional, but it will really make caramel making much easier. Unless you've decided to take up professional candy making, you can buy the cheapest one for less than $20, and it will work just fine.

Canoe pan: If you want to try making Twinkies, this will make your life much easier. You can use the pan as a substitute for a muffin pan in the future.

Cookie cutter, round: Many of my recipes here call for a round cookie cutter, but a two-inch-diameter juice glass will do. Whichever cookie cutter you use, remember to dip it in flour as you cut; when making chocolate cookies, dip the cutter in cocoa powder.

(Good) cookie sheets: My teenager once did a science experiment in which she made chocolate chip cookies on a variety of cookie sheets—disposable ones, inexpensive metal ones, and fancy insulated versions—to see if there was any substantial difference. The cookies were all delicious! But the insulated sheets made for more even browning, and I recommend this type if you bake often. I also love the large professional-style baking sheets, which fit far more cookies and also bake evenly. (If you live in a tiny apartment with a tiny stove, be sure to measure your oven width and depth before you buy one of these larger baking sheets.)

Dough scoop: I discovered this tool when I was baking large quantities of cookies and cupcakes for my daughter's bat mitzvah, and I really could not believe I had lived without one for so long. A melon baller or trigger-handled ice cream scoop, which comes in a variety of sizes, will provide you with uniform-size cookies and will cut the bowl-to-cookie-sheet transfer process in half. Who wants cookie dough under the fingernails anyway? Large scoops are great for scooping and plopping muffin and cupcake batter. Put them on your birthday wish list.

Measuring cups: The web is full of all sorts of fancy measuring cups made up of different materials, colors, and the like, but I think the supermarket versions are perfectly fine. The key is to have a stainless steel set for dry ingredients and a glass one (I love my old Pyrex one from Gristedes in New York City) for measuring liquids. Do not switch them up while baking, or you will not get accurate measurements.

Mixer: Yes, I love my countertop mixer: a heavy, expensive, and counter space–hogging luxury item that really is a must-have for the frequent baker. Its greatest asset is the time it saves, because it creams your butter and sugar while you mix up your dry ingredients, ready your pans, and maybe yell at one of your kids to do her math homework. It is the BMW of kitchen tools and, with a few attachments, can do a ton of other tasks, such as grind meat and make pasta. However, I still keep my standard electric hand mixer around, which I prefer for whipping egg whites and other small-scale projects.

Offset spatula: An offset spatula is another useful and inexpensive tool. With thin or fragile baked goods, the design of this tool, which has a stainless steel "busy" end and a plastic or a wooden handle, is perfect for removing your items from the tray. It is also great for transferring cookies from your rolling surface to the pan and, as a bonus, for scraping up bits of whatever on the counter.

Parchment paper: I am a firm believer in parchment paper over greased baking sheets, no matter what a recipe calls for. It prevents a big mess and helps things brown evenly. The best resource, other than your local grocery, is CulinaryDistrict.com, the website of the legendary Surfas culinary store in Los Angeles. You can buy paper by the hundred-sheet pack and in small packs of precut rounds for cake pans, ending up with enough sheets to last you forever (or through the writing of one cookbook).

(Good heavy) rolling pin: I cannot tell you how much time I've wasted, how many tears I've cried using my old wooden rolling pin for rolling out dough. It wasn't heavy enough to get the dough as thin as I needed, and it was too

A Few Notes About Technique

Baking, unlike cooking, calls for precision. Precision is why some bakers rely completely on scales rather than on cups and spoons, and lack of precision explains why your cookies, which you made with a rounded teaspoon of this or mixed up with ice cold butter, never look and taste as good as your mother-in-law's version. You can skip a chile here or a spice there when making soup, but a dough without the proper combination of ingredients is very likely to disappoint. I have lived my entire life chafing at authority, but when it comes to cake, I do what Martha Stewart says.

Unless a recipe indicates otherwise, your ingredients need to be at room temperature. As the amazing baker Gail Dosik, the genius behind One Tough Cookie, Inc., explains: "In baked goods like cakes and cookies, room temperature butter makes a homogeneous dough or batter, because as the butter is creamed with the sugar, the edges of the sugar crystals are coated evenly with the butter, the beginning of a great cake structure or 'crumb.' The better the incorporation, the better the crumb." Milk, cream, and eggs also need to be at room temperature, because room-temperature butter will just seize up and lump if cold eggs or milk are added to it. Taste your batter as you go: if it isn't delicious, chances are your cookie won't be either. Stop fretting about salmonella; a bite of cookie dough isn't likely to bring you low. Texture, however, can be deceiving; sometimes batter looks too gloppy or thin but will be right once baked. Be sure to make things the size the recipe indicates, or you may end up with giant cookies with soft centers and burned edges.

Finally, sometimes things just fail. Don't get upset. In truth, everyone prefers a sweet from home to a store-bought version, even if your creation looks like it's been mauled by a marsupial. They will forgive you. Remember, frosting covers a multitude of kitchen sins. As do sprinkles.

short, so its handles always got in the way of a full roll. Go to your cookware store and try different models. I love my plastic, handleless version designed for making fondant, because, as opposed to wooden models, the dough comes off easily at cleanup time, and the lack of handles means I can roll out large dough portions. But, different strokes . . .

Rubber spatulas: The rubber spatula is bar none my favorite kitchen tool. I have four in various sizes, and I use them in place of wooden spoons for almost all my baking needs, and in many cases for savory dishes. The flexible head makes scraping dough from the mixing bowl a breeze, and you get every last bit. Rubber spatulas are easy to wash and, unlike wooden spoons, can go in the dishwasher.

Scale: There are many bakers who believe that weighing rather than measuring ingredients is the only way to get truly accurate amounts. Rose Levy Beranbaum, the author of *The Cake Bible*, uses weight measurements in her books—because you really haven't lived until you've weighed an egg yolk. You can probably skip those lovely electronic kitchen scales on the market, even though some are really great and affordable. But you should at least invest in an inexpensive postage scale for measuring out chocolate. It will come in handy for other kitchen projects as well as for weighing your holiday cards.

Sifter: The sifter is a controversial item, because many bakers believe that a standard kitchen strainer works just fine as the go-between for your dry ingredients and the mixing bowl. Others prefer to simply aerate their flour with a fork. But the sifter performs valuable functions: it aerates dry ingredients so they produce a lighter product, and it incorporates all dry ingredients together so you don't get a clump of salt or baking powder somewhere. I have my mother-in-law's sifter from the 1950s and love it dearly; newer ones can have arms that stick.

Whisk: The balloon shape of a wire whisk helps to aerate eggs and creams and is much more effective at helping you integrate dry ingredients than a wooden spoon; it can also be used in place of a sifter. A crossover tool from baking to cooking, at least one whisk is good to have on hand.

Wire rack: A nice sturdy wire rack for cooling items is better than a flimsy one and is absolutely needed for cookie baking. Cakes, too, do better cooling on this surface, which permits air to enter beneath the hot pan. They are, admittedly, a pill to clean; I recommend a toothbrush, preferably paired with a teenager.

Chapter 1
—

CLASSIC COOKIES

My first word, according to my mother, was *cookie*. The first cookies I remember were tiny chocolate ones, sold in a little brown box with an animal face on their front. I also recall animal crackers iced with pink frosting and dotted with sprinkles, my grandmother's royal fans (brown sugar cookies intricately painted with egg yolks doctored with food coloring), and, of course, freshly baked Toll House cookies, snatched right off the pan, the chocolate burning my lips. The cookie recipes included here feature the flavors and varieties of the most popular commercial cookies—cookies that prompt a wave of food memories from coast to coast.

The very word *cookie* was likely brought to the United States by the Dutch, derived from their word *koeptje*, which means "small cake." It seems new Americans were far more jazzed about using Dutch words than those of the British, whose habits and customs they were trying to shake off, including the British insistence on calling sweet cakes "biscuits."

Most cookies begin their journey from disparate ingredients to your tummy in relatively the same manner: by creaming butter and sugar loudly together in the mixer; adding some eggs as a binding agent, along with flavors (often vanilla); and finally mixing in flour and some baking soda, baking powder, or both, to help the cookies rise. A cookie is, at base, a fairly simple confection.

Mrs. Fields stand-alone cookie stores began to pop up in the late 1970s, solidifying the cookie's clear slide from midday treat, à la English tea, to an anytime, anywhere snacking staple. The Girl Scouts, as you no doubt know, also got in on the act, beginning with troop moms volunteering to teach the young ladies how to bake. The organization first realized it was onto something lucrative in 1917, when a troop in Muskogee, Oklahoma, sold their goods in a high school cafeteria. Soon Girl Scout troops began selling their cookies, under the supervision of moms, sealed in wax paper bags.

It seems appropriate to share in a moment of thanks that some entrepreneurial prowess provided the rest of us with a bounty of annual treats. Those boxes may have had humble origins, but now we pile them up around office desks, bedroom sets, and kitchen tables. Who among us has not raised a fist to defend the last Samoa?

So here we are: the cookie, once an exotic midday treat, has evolved into its own food group, with every imaginable variation available on the grocery shelf. I would not consider packing a lunch, even for an adult, without a cookie of some sort that can be eaten in whatever ritualistic fashion, frosting first, sprinkles last, dipped or undipped.

Pour a glass of milk. Let's get started.

LEMON COOLERS

HANDS-ON TIME
15 minutes

TOTAL TIME
30 minutes

Lemon coolers are a bit of an underappreciated sleeper cookie, but they are deeply beloved by those who like their cookie with a citrus twist. The recipe is also quick and easy, unless you make the error I did at one point, which was to use one stick of butter rather than one and a half sticks. (This error may or may not have crept in because while I was baking, I was also drinking gin, folding laundry, and pondering the upper-body strength of an actress on *Modern Family*, leading to a bowl of powdery mess.) When the correct butter quantity is used, these cookies are light and delicious and very close in texture to the Sunshine Biscuits original. They sort of melt in the mouth, which is how I remember them from the first time I tried them, in the cookie dish of a friend of my great-grandmother. This old woman spoke only German and didn't let us wear shoes on the carpet. Compared with the rest of the visit, the cookies melting on our tongues were a bit of comfort.

Makes approximately 30 cookies

¾ cup (1½ sticks) unsalted butter, softened
1 teaspoon lemon extract
1 teaspoon freshly grated lemon zest
1½ cups all-purpose flour
1⅓ cups powdered sugar
1 teaspoon baking powder

1 Preheat the oven to 325°F. Line two baking sheets with parchment paper.

2 In the bowl of a heavy-duty stand mixer, beat the butter on medium speed for 1 minute, or until creamy. Add the lemon extract and zest, and mix for another 30 seconds.

3 In a separate bowl, sift together the flour, 1 cup of the powdered sugar, and the baking powder. With the mixer on low speed, gradually add the flour mixture to the butter mixture in three or four batches, mixing just until all the dry ingredients are incorporated.

4 Using a small trigger-handled scoop or a spoon, place the dough in quarter-size rounds 2 inches apart on the prepared baking sheets.

5 Bake for 14 to 16 minutes, or until the cookies are set and just beginning to brown around the edges. Let the cookies cool on a wire rack for 5 minutes.

6 Dust the cookies with the remaining powdered sugar and let cool completely. Store in an airtight container for up to 3 days.

THIN MINTS

HANDS-ON TIME
30 minutes

TOTAL TIME
2 hours

Who among us has not plowed through an entire sleeve of Thin Mints right from the freezer, perhaps while watching old *Friends* episodes at three a.m.? When I was a Girl Scout, my parents ordered six boxes of these for our house alone. As with many of these recipes, the flavor profile will match the cookies of your youth, absent the snap that comes from stabilizers. (Ideally, the cookies should be baked as long as possible without burning, which can help with the snappiness.) You also need to be careful not to make your blobs of dough too big, or you will have something more like an undersized brownie than a Thin Mint—the equivalent of a twenty-four-year-old Girl Scout knocking at the door looking for a beer. *Makes approximately 30 cookies*

for the cookie

½ cup (1 stick) unsalted butter, softened

1 cup sugar

1½ teaspoons peppermint extract (spearmint will do as well) (see Note)

1 large egg

1¾ cups all-purpose flour

¼ cup Dutch-processed cocoa powder, such as Droste

¼ teaspoon baking powder

¼ teaspoon salt

for the chocolate coating

2½ cups (15 ounces) semisweet chocolate morsels

¾ cup (1½ sticks) unsalted butter, plus 1 tablespoon to keep coating smooth (optional)

½ teaspoon peppermint extract (spearmint will do as well)

1 Preheat the oven to 350°F. Line two baking sheets with parchment paper.

2 Make the cookie dough: In the bowl of a heavy-duty stand mixer, beat the ½ cup butter and the sugar together on medium speed until light and fluffy, about two minutes. Add the mint extract and the egg, and mix until fully incorporated, scraping down the sides and the bottom of the bowl as you go.

3 In a large bowl, whisk together the flour, cocoa, baking powder, and salt. With the mixer on low speed, gradually add the flour mixture to the butter mixture in three batches, stopping to scrape the bowl, until all ingredients are thoroughly mixed.

4 Using a small trigger-handled scoop or a spoon, place the dough in quarter-size rounds 2 inches apart on the prepared baking sheets. Bake for 14 to 16 minutes, until the cookies are set and firm in appearance. Let the cookies cool completely on a wire rack.

5 Make the chocolate coating: In a large microwave-safe bowl (see Note), microwave the chocolate and the ¾ cup of butter on medium heat for 1 minute, or until melted, stirring every 30 seconds. Stir in the mint extract until the mixture is completely smooth and easily drips off the back of a spoon.

RECIPE CONTINUES

NOTE: If you use peppermint oil instead of peppermint extract, use a third of the stated amount, as the oil is far more potent.

6 Carefully dip the top of each cooled cookie into the coating, allowing the excess chocolate to run off. (If the chocolate begins to set before all the cookies are coated, add 1 tablespoon of butter to the chocolate mixture in the bowl and microwave on medium heat for 10 more seconds until the mixture is smooth again.) Place the cookies back onto the baking sheets and let them rest for 45 minutes to 1 hour, or until the chocolate is set. Store in an airtight container for 3 days, or in the freezer for 1 month.

NOTE: I cannot overstate the importance of dry bowls and utensils when melting chocolate—even a tiny amount of water left in the bowl will cause the chocolate to seize and become hard and useless. Also, overheating chocolate is a risk because it will dry out, but you can fix that error by adding more fat, like butter, during the melting process. Different grades of chocolate overheat at different temperatures, so be aware—the higher the quality, the higher the heat it can take.

GINGERSNAPS

HANDS-ON TIME
15 minutes

TOTAL TIME
30 minutes

There are as many types of commercial gingersnaps as there are stars in the sky, and everyone has his or her favorite kind. Some appreciate the small versions that are almost unsnappable until they have rested in the mouth a bit, brown sugar dissolving on the tongue while you listen to the latest Beyoncé song. Others prefer their gingersnaps big and chewy, like the sort sold in bags rather than boxes. Everyone agrees that gingersnaps must taste very much of ginger, preferably in a way that almost burns the mouth. This version of the gingersnap—the cookie that finds its roots in German bakeries (possibly beginning with medieval monks in Franconia)—splits the difference: it's on the small size but is also somewhat chewy, a texture my office mates could not stop raving about (until I had to ask them to go away so I could write about the fiscal cliff). I think you'll find it a great marriage of texture and bite, with a tad of black pepper added for extra kick. Your coworkers or guests will beg you for more, too. *Makes approximately 40 cookies*

¾ cup (1½ sticks) unsalted butter, softened

¼ cup shortening

1¼ cups (packed) dark brown sugar

¼ cup unsulfured molasses

1 large egg

2 cups all-purpose flour

1 teaspoon baking soda

½ teaspoon salt

1 teaspoon cinnamon

2 teaspoons ground ginger

¼ teaspoon ground cloves

¼ teaspoon black pepper (preferably freshly ground)

1 Preheat the oven to 350°F. Line two baking sheets with parchment paper.

2 In the bowl of a heavy-duty stand mixer, beat the butter, shortening, brown sugar, and molasses together on medium speed until creamy. Add the egg and mix for another 30 seconds, or until smooth.

3 In a separate bowl, whisk together the flour, baking soda, salt, cinnamon, ginger, cloves, and black pepper. With the mixer on low speed, gradually add the flour mixture to the brown sugar–molasses mixture in three batches, mixing just until all the dry ingredients are incorporated. Refrigerate the dough for 30 minutes.

4 Using a small trigger-handled scoop or a spoon, place the dough in quarter-size rounds 2 inches apart on the prepared baking sheets. Bake for 14 to 16 minutes, or until the cookies are set, rotating the pans midbake.

5 Let the cookies cool a bit on the pans before turning out onto a wire rack to cool. Store in an airtight container for up to 3 days.

SAMOAS

HANDS-ON TIME
55 minutes

TOTAL TIME
2 hours,
15 minutes

Although Samoas have been offered by the Girl Scouts only since the mid-1970s, they are the second most popular Girl Scout cookie, trailing only the addictive Thin Mint. The popularity of Samoas is especially impressive, since they are not among the handful of cookies that official Girl Scout commercial bakers are required to make. A complex amalgam of caramel, coconut, and chocolate, the Samoa is the art-student boyfriend of confections, a layered, multifarious affair, while the Thin Mint is the sexy accountant—reliable, easy, a natural pleasure.

You won't want to embark on making a batch of Samoas the morning of a birthday party lest you end up frantic and nervous with bits of caramel in your hair. The recipe is not so difficult as it is time consuming, with several steps along the way. However, the payoff is huge—butter, cream, and more butter are in every bite—and you will soon understand why eating a single box can bring you up one pant size. This recipe is complicated enough without adding the original Samoa hole in the middle; I'm hoping you can live with that!

Makes approximately 40 cookies

for the cookie

- ¾ cup (1½ sticks) unsalted butter, softened
- ¾ cup granulated sugar
- ¾ cup (packed) light brown sugar
- 1 large egg
- 1 teaspoon vanilla extract
- 2¼ cups all-purpose flour
- ¾ teaspoon salt
- ¾ teaspoon baking powder
- ½ teaspoon baking soda

1 Preheat the oven to 350°F. Line two baking sheets with parchment paper.

2 Make the cookie dough: In the bowl of a heavy-duty stand mixer, cream the ¾ cup butter, ¾ cup granulated sugar, and brown sugar together on medium speed for 2 minutes, or until fluffy. Add the egg and mix for another minute. Scrape down the sides of the bowl, add the vanilla, and continue to mix for 10 seconds.

3 In a medium bowl, whisk together the flour, ¾ teaspoon salt, baking powder, and baking soda. With the mixer running, slowly add the flour mixture to the butter mixture in three or four batches, mixing until all the ingredients are incorporated. Scrape down the sides and bottom of the bowl, and mix for another 10 to 15 seconds to combine.

4 Using a small trigger-handled scoop or a spoon, place rounded tablespoons of the cookie dough 2 inches apart on the prepared

RECIPE CONTINUES

for the coconut

1½ cups packed sweetened coconut

for the chocolate ganache

⅓ cup heavy whipping cream

2 cups (12 ounces) semisweet chocolate morsels

for the caramel topping

½ cup (1 stick) unsalted butter

1 cup sugar

½ cup heavy whipping cream

½ teaspoon salt

NOTE: Carefully watch your coconut while it's roasting so it doesn't burn.

NOTE: Be careful not to let the caramel overcook—you want it to be pulling away from the pan, not overly dark. David Lebovitz, the great American baker now based in Paris, gives an extensive tutorial on caramel making on his website, for those of you who may be interested.

baking sheets. Bake for 15 to 17 minutes, or until the cookies are golden brown, rotating the pans after 7 minutes. Allow the cookies to cool completely on wire racks. (Do not turn off the oven.)

5 Toast the coconut: Spread the coconut on a rimmed baking sheet. Bake 10 minutes, or until golden, stirring every 3 minutes (see Note).

6 Make the chocolate ganache: In a large microwave-safe bowl, microwave the cream and chocolate morsels on high heat for 2 minutes, stirring every 30 seconds, until melted. Let cool for 2 minutes. Turn the cooled cookies upside down and spread a thin layer of chocolate on each cookie. (Reserve the remaining chocolate.) Wait 30 minutes, or until the chocolate is set, before turning the cookies right side up.

7 Make the caramel: In a medium saucepan, combine the ½ cup butter and the 1 cup sugar and cook over medium-high heat, stirring frequently, until the mixture begins to boil. Continue to cook, stirring constantly, for 5 to 7 minutes, or until golden and smooth (see Note). (The mixture may separate, so keep stirring as necessary.) Remove from the heat and slowly stir in the heavy cream and salt. Stir continuously as the caramel bubbles, until smooth. Let cool for 20 minutes.

8 Spread a spoonful of caramel over each cookie (see Note) and sprinkle generously with toasted coconut. (Unused caramel can be refrigerated in an airtight container for up to 5 days.)

9 Reheat the remaining chocolate ganache in a medium microwave-safe bowl for 10 to 15 seconds, until melted. Spoon the warm ganache into a disposable piping bag or plastic bag. Snip the end of the bag to create a small hole, and top each cookie with thin drizzles of chocolate. Let sit for 10 minutes. Store in an airtight container for up to 3 days.

NOTE: To make for an easier cleanup, place some newspaper under your baking sheets before adding the caramel and coconut.

FROSTED OATMEAL COOKIES

HANDS-ON TIME
25 minutes

TOTAL TIME
1 hour,
10 minutes

Fans of oatmeal cookies can debate endlessly whether the best versions are chewy or crispy, giant or simply large. One colleague becomes almost weepy talking about his mother's cookies, which the two of them would eat together when they both had insomnia. "I have this memory of sitting at the bottom of the stairs, and we each had a couple of cookies together," he recalled. "Frosted, they had to be frosted!"

This recipe will be preferred by those who love their oatmeal cookies big, sweet, and chewy, much like the Archway brand I grew up with. I use a large scoop to make them, but my first batch had some brown sugar hot spots that may have resulted from undermixing.

Makes approximately 40 cookies

for the cookie

1 cup (2 sticks) salted butter, softened

1 cup (packed) light brown sugar

¾ cup granulated sugar

2 large eggs

2 teaspoons vanilla extract

2 cups all-purpose flour

1½ cups old-fashioned oats

1 teaspoon baking soda

1½ teaspoons baking powder

1 teaspoon salt

½ teaspoon cinnamon

for the frosting

2½ cups powdered sugar

3 tablespoons whole milk

1 Preheat the oven to 350°F. Line two baking sheets with parchment paper.

2 Make the cookie dough: In the bowl of a heavy-duty stand mixer, cream the butter, brown sugar, and granulated sugar together on medium speed for 1 minute, or until light and fluffy. Add the eggs one at a time, mixing just until combined. Add the vanilla, and mix for another 3 to 5 seconds.

3 In a medium bowl, stir together the flour, oats, baking soda, baking powder, salt, and cinnamon. With the mixer on low speed, gradually add the flour mixture to the butter mixture in three batches, roughly a minute each, mixing just until all the dry ingredients are incorporated.

4 Using a small trigger-handled scoop or a spoon, place quarter-size rounds of dough 2 inches apart on the prepared baking sheets. Bake for 13 to 15 minutes, or until the cookies are set and just beginning to brown around the edges. Let the cookies cool completely on wire racks.

5 Make the frosting: In a small bowl, whisk together the powdered sugar and milk. Transfer to a piping bag, then drizzle a generous amount of frosting over each cookie. Let the frosting set before storing in an airtight container for up to 3 days.

PECAN SANDIES

The Pecan Sandie fan living in a world of chocolate lovers is like a Cardinals fan sitting in Wrigley Field, trying to be inconspicuous as she roots for her beloved team. My grandmother's version, which she made each holiday season, was a rich sugar cookie topped with a single pecan, which I would promptly remove and stick under a chair cushion, where it would be discovered around Easter. "Those are twelve dollars a pound!" Grandma would exclaim when she found the offending nuts, which meant nothing to me for approximately twenty years. In time, I learned to appreciate both the sandy quality of these cookies and the deep nutty flavor. *Makes approximately 25 cookies*

1 cup (2 sticks) salted butter, softened

¾ cup sugar

1 large egg yolk

3 cups all-purpose flour, plus more for rolling out the dough

½ teaspoon salt

½ teaspoon baking powder

1 cup finely chopped pecans

NOTE: This recipe comes closer to the commercial version, with chopped pecans throughout. You will need strong arms and a good rolling pin to roll this dough out. If you fail, or just don't feel like it, fashion the dough into balls, flatten them with the bottom of a glass, set them an inch apart on the baking sheet, and call it a day. They won't be as pretty, but they will definitely be as tasty.

1 In the bowl of a heavy-duty stand mixer, beat the butter and sugar together on medium speed for about 1 minute, or until light and fluffy. Add the egg yolk and mix just until combined.

2 In a medium bowl, whisk together the flour, salt, and baking powder. With the mixer on low speed, slowly add the flour mixture to the butter mixture in three batches, scraping down the sides of the bowl and mixing just until combined. Add the pecans, and mix on low for 5 seconds, or just until the pecans are evenly incorporated. The mixture should be crumbly but still hold together when squeezed. Turn the dough out onto a piece of plastic wrap, shape into a 1-inch disk, and refrigerate for 1 hour.

3 Preheat the oven to 350°F. Line two baking sheets with parchment paper.

4 Remove the dough from the refrigerator and let rest at room temperature for 10 to 15 minutes. Roll out the dough on a lightly floured surface to a thickness of about ½ inch. Using a 2-inch round cutter, cut out the cookies and place them 1 inch apart on the prepared baking sheet.

5 Bake the cookies for 12 to 14 minutes, or until lightly golden around the edges. Let the cookies cool completely on a wire rack. Store in an airtight container at room temperature for up to 3 days.

CHIPS AHOY!

HANDS-ON TIME
30 minutes

TOTAL TIME
1 hour,
30 minutes

Is there really anything more controversial than a chocolate chip cookie? Entire newspaper articles have been devoted to the soft-versus-crisp dichotomy. Everyone has their preferred version, both homemade and store bought, and is utterly convinced that their favorite is the best. Our recipe is the soft version, the "chewy" varietal, and the key to maintaining the proper texture is a low oven temperature and a longish cooking time. Of course, on many levels, Chips Ahoy! was never the grandest brand of chocolate chip cookies—that spot is reserved on the commercial level for Mrs. Fields, and for the Toll House cookie recipe when it comes to your own oven.

Makes approximately 80 cookies

1 cup (2 sticks) salted butter, softened

1 cup (packed) light brown sugar

¾ cup granulated sugar

2 large eggs

2 teaspoons vanilla extract

3½ cups all-purpose flour

1½ teaspoons baking powder

1 teaspoon baking soda

1 teaspoon salt

2½ cups (15 ounces) milk chocolate morsels

1 Preheat the oven to 315°F. Line two baking sheets with parchment paper.

2 In the bowl of a heavy-duty stand mixer, cream the butter, brown sugar, and granulated sugar together on medium speed for 1 minute, or until light and fluffy. Add the eggs one at a time and mix just until combined, scraping down the sides and bottom of the bowl. Add the vanilla and continue to mix for 3 to 5 seconds.

3 In a medium bowl, whisk together the flour, baking powder, baking soda, and salt. With the mixer on low speed, slowly add the flour mixture into the butter mixture in batches, mixing just until all the dry ingredients are incorporated. Scrape the bowl again, add the chocolate, and mix just until the morsels are evenly distributed.

4 Using a small trigger-handled scoop or a spoon, place the dough in small rounded mounds, about 2 teaspoons each, 2 inches apart on the prepared baking sheets. Bake the cookies, one pan at a time, for 19 to 21 minutes, or until the cookies are golden brown. (If you can't set out all your dough for baking at once, store the unbaked cookie dough in the refrigerator between batches.)

5 Let the cookies cool completely on a wire rack. Store in an airtight container for up to 3 days.

BISCOFF

I am always happy to find myself on certain flights—they tend to be from Washington to Detroit—in which the in-flight treat is a Biscoff cookie, a treat that actually traces its history directly to the sky. The cookies, which are crispy and taste heavily of brown sugar, were created in 1932 in Belgium, where they are still made by Lotus Bakeries. Legend has it that the cookies were discovered by an airline food supplier during a trip to Belgium in 1984. He immediately purchased them for his airline, and travelers have been associating those cookies with edited movies and coffee with powdered creamer ever since.

This version takes some liberties with the shape but preserves the excellent brown sugar snap. The cookies are slightly richer because this version, unlike the commercial one, uses butter. The next time I have a flight on a noncookie airline, I will bring a batch of these tucked into my carry-on and share them with the person next to me, provided he or she is NOT watching an action movie without headphones or taking up two armrests, thus creating my own interpretation of the "mile-high club." *Makes approximately 40 cookies*

1 cup (2 sticks) salted
    butter, softened
2 cups (packed) dark
    brown sugar
2 large eggs
1 teaspoon vanilla extract
3 cups all-purpose flour
½ teaspoon baking soda
½ teaspoon baking
    powder
½ teaspoon cinnamon

1 Preheat the oven to 325°F. Line two baking sheets with parchment paper.

2 In the bowl of a heavy-duty stand mixer, cream the butter and brown sugar together on medium speed for 1 minute, or until light and fluffy. Add the eggs one at a time, mixing just until each is incorporated. Add the vanilla, and mix for another 3 to 5 seconds.

3 In a medium bowl, whisk together the flour, baking soda, baking powder, and cinnamon. With the mixer on low speed, add the flour mixture to the butter mixture in batches, mixing just until all the dry ingredients are incorporated.

4 Using a small trigger-handled scoop or a spoon, place quarter-size rounds of the dough 2 inches apart on the prepared baking sheets. Bake for 12 to 14 minutes, or until the cookies are set. Let cool completely on wire racks. Store in an airtight container for up to 3 days.

LORNA DOONE SHORTBREAD COOKIES

HANDS-ON TIME
20 minutes

TOTAL TIME
2 hours

One really has to love a cookie named after the main character of an English novel set in the seventeenth century, an heiress resisting a loveless marriage. My own associations with this treat are very specific, yet no less odd: after 9/11, the entire New York City government began functioning out of a pier in midtown Manhattan, where the City Hall press was also housed. Each day scores of volunteers would come to the pier to hand out delicious donated food to City Hall staffers. Meanwhile, way on the other side of the facility, the reporters were given bruised apples and packages of Lorna Doones. I cannot eat one without thinking of that time, and yet the comfort of their buttery, inoffensive salve sticks with me still. *Makes approximately 40 cookies*

1½ cups (3 sticks) salted butter, softened
¾ cup sugar
3 cups all-purpose flour
¾ cup cornstarch
½ teaspoon baking soda
½ teaspoon salt

NOTE: I love this recipe because I tend to cut dough on the thick side, which works well for this cookie. (Watch for overbrowning.)

1 In the bowl of a heavy-duty stand mixer, cream the butter and sugar together on medium speed for 1 minute.

2 In a medium bowl, whisk together the flour, cornstarch, baking soda, and salt. With the mixer on low speed, add the flour mixture to the butter mixture in batches, mixing just until all the dry ingredients are incorporated—the mixture should be crumbly but hold together when squeezed. Turn the dough out onto a piece of plastic wrap, shape into a 1-inch disk, and refrigerate for 1 hour.

3 Preheat the oven to 325°F. Line two baking sheets with parchment paper.

4 Remove the dough from the refrigerator and let sit at room temperature for 10 minutes. Roll the dough out to a thickness of about ¼ inch. Using a pizza cutter or bench scraper, first cut the dough into 1½-inch strips, then cut each strip into 1½-inch squares (see Note).

5 Set the squares 1 inch apart on the prepared baking sheets and bake, one pan at a time, for 25 to 30 minutes, or until the cookies are set and just beginning to brown around the edges. Let cool completely on a wire rack. Store in an airtight container for up to 1 week.

ICED MOLASSES COOKIES

HANDS-ON TIME
25 minutes
TOTAL TIME
1 hour

These cookies are both delicate and rich, with odd hints of apple. It's often hard to find molasses year-round, but it's always available in wintertime, when the aroma is, for many Americans, the smell of Christmas.

The first time I tasted the batter for these cookies, I was a bit knocked over by the sheer molasses-ness of it all, but the molasses flavor becomes somewhat subdued during the baking and is tamed into submission by the icing. *Makes approximately 60 cookies*

for the cookie

- 1 cup (2 sticks) unsalted butter, softened
- 1 cup (packed) dark brown sugar
- 1 cup molasses
- 2 large eggs
- 1 teaspoon vanilla extract
- 3 cups all-purpose flour
- ½ teaspoon baking soda
- 1¼ teaspoons baking powder
- ½ teaspoon salt
- ¼ teaspoon cinnamon

for the icing

- 4 cups powdered sugar
- ½ cup whole milk

1 Preheat the oven to 375°F. Line two baking sheets with parchment paper.

2 Make the cookie dough: In the bowl of a heavy-duty stand mixer, cream the butter, brown sugar, and molasses together on medium speed for 1 minute, or until light and fluffy. Add the eggs one at a time, mixing just until combined. Add the vanilla, and mix for another 3 to 5 seconds.

3 In a medium bowl, whisk together the flour, baking soda, baking powder, salt, and cinnamon. With the mixer on low speed, gradually add the flour mixture to the butter mixture in three batches, mixing just until all the dry ingredients are incorporated.

4 Using a small trigger-handled scoop or a spoon, place quarter-size rounds of the dough 2 inches apart on the prepared baking sheets. Bake for 10 to 12 minutes, or until the cookies are set. Let the cookies sit on the pan for a few minutes before turning them onto a cooling rack—they are delicate, so they need an extra minute, but not too long or they will stick to the pan. Transfer and let cool completely on wire racks before icing.

5 Make the icing: In a small, shallow bowl, whisk together the powdered sugar and milk. Dip the top of each cooled cookie in the icing, allowing the excess to run off into the bowl. Place the cookies icing side up on baking sheets. Let the icing set completely before storing in an airtight container for up to 3 days.

TAGALONGS

HANDS-ON TIME
45 minutes

TOTAL TIME
3 hours,
30 minutes

The third-biggest seller among Girl Scout cookies, these creamy cookies are popular among peanut butter fans, even though peanut butter cookie purists usually do not care for the involvement of chocolate. When I took my first batch to the office—I can't lie—there was some controversy: Wasn't the peanut butter meant to go all the way across the cookie? (No, it's more of a dollop.) Are they really supposed to be covered with this much chocolate? (Well, I was heavy handed.) Tagalong fans, less populous than the Thin Mint freaks but equally passionate, are relentless in their critiques of homemade versions: "Too much peanut butter!" "Not enough!" But these cookies, the baked version of a pimped-out peanut butter cup, make up for whatever authenticity shortcomings with their indulgent richness and peanut flavor. *Makes approximately 40 cookies*

for the cookie

1 cup (2 sticks) salted
    butter, softened
¾ cup granulated sugar
¾ cup (packed) light
    brown sugar
1 large egg
1 teaspoon vanilla extract
3½ cups all-purpose flour
1 teaspoon baking powder
1 teaspoon baking soda
½ teaspoon salt

for the filling

2 cups smooth commercial
    peanut butter, like Jif
    (do not use natural
    peanut butter)

1 Make the cookie dough: In the bowl of a heavy-duty stand mixer, mix the 1 cup butter and the granulated and brown sugars together on medium speed until light and fluffy, about 1 minute. Add the egg and vanilla and mix just until combined.

2 In a medium bowl, whisk together the flour, baking powder, baking soda, and salt. With the mixer on low speed, slowly add the flour mixture to the butter mixture in batches, mixing just until all the dry ingredients are incorporated. Cover with plastic wrap, placing the plastic directly on the cookie dough, and refrigerate for 20 minutes.

3 Preheat the oven to 350°F. Line a baking sheet with parchment paper.

4 Using a small trigger-handled scoop or a spoon, place rounded tablespoons of the cookie dough 2 inches apart on the prepared baking sheet. (Return the raw dough to the refrigerator until ready to bake.) Use the back of a spoon to flatten the cookie and create a small indentation across the top. Bake for 15 to 17 minutes, or until set and lightly golden brown. Let the cookies cool completely on wire racks.

for the chocolate coating

¾ cup (1½ sticks) salted
    butter, softened
4 cups (24 ounces) milk
    chocolate morsels

5 Make the filling: Place the peanut butter into a piping bag (a disposable freezer bag with the corner cut will work) and pipe a small amount, about 2 teaspoons, in an oblong dollop on the top of each cookie. Refrigerate the peanut butter-topped cookies for 2 hours.

6 Place 2 lightly greased wire racks over rimmed baking sheets lined with parchment or wax paper.

7 Make the chocolate coating: Place the ¾ cup butter in a medium-large heatproof bowl. In a small saucepan, bring 2 to 3 inches of water to a boil over medium heat. Turn off the heat and place the bowl of butter over the saucepan. Stir constantly until the butter melts. Pour the chocolate morsels into the melted butter, stirring constantly until the chocolate melts and the mixture is smooth.

8 Use your hands to dip each cookie in the chocolate: start with the bottom of the cookie, scraping off any excess chocolate on the edge of the bowl, then turn the cookie over to dip the top. (Use your fingers to smooth chocolate over any uncovered surface.) Place the dipped cookies on the wire rack to set. Let the chocolate coating set completely. Store in an airtight container for up to 4 days.

NILLA WAFERS

HANDS-ON TIME
20 minutes
TOTAL TIME
45 minutes

The first time I made this cookie, it was one of the best sugar cookies I had tasted, ever. But it was not a Nilla Wafer. I took it to the office, and everyone agreed that, while my version was great, it was not quite right. It was a bit of a texture issue— Nilla Wafers, often the go-to cookie for the preschool set, have a funny snap and yet crumble so deliciously in milk. But also, Nilla Wafers really taste of vanilla. It was back to the kitchen, where I added more vanilla and tweaked the ratio of flour to fat until I created a cookie that had both that unique texture and enough vanilla to distinguish it from mere butter or sugar cookies. *Makes approximately 90 cookies*

½ cup (1 stick) salted
  butter, softened
1 cup sugar
2 large eggs
2 tablespoons vanilla
  extract
2½ cups all-purpose flour
1 teaspoon baking powder

NOTE: If you pipe the dough from a pastry bag into little fluffy disks, the cookies will look perfect, but you can also use a small spoon to turn out the dough.

1 Preheat the oven to 315°F. Line two baking sheets with parchment paper.

2 In the bowl of a heavy-duty stand mixer, cream the butter and sugar together on medium speed until light and fluffy, about 1 minute. Add the eggs one at a time and mix on medium-high speed until the mixture is thickened and pale yellow. Scrape the sides and the bottom of the bowl, add the vanilla, and continue to mix until smooth.

3 In a separate bowl, whisk together the flour and the baking powder. With the mixer on low speed, slowly mix the dry mixture into the butter mixture, just until all the dry ingredients are incorporated.

4 Transfer the dough to a piping bag and pipe quarter-size rounds of dough (see Note) set 2 inches apart on the prepared baking pans. Bake the cookies for 18 to 20 minutes, or until golden brown. Allow the cookies to cool on wire racks for 5 minutes, then transfer to an airtight container to finish cooling. Store in an airtight container for up to 3 days.

FAMOUS CHOCOLATE WAFERS

HANDS-ON TIME
30 minutes

TOTAL TIME
2 hours,
15 minutes

Many people use these delicate wafers as the basis of a piecrust, or crush them into other desserts. In my house they played a starring role, and my mother kept a sheet of them hidden in the pantry behind the dog food, lest they be stolen. The cookies are almost sandy to the bite; if dunked in milk, they instantly dissolve into a chocolate paste. The back of the Wafers box suggested fashioning a giant log held together by whipped cream; Mom took a shortcut simply by covering individual cookies with the cream.

This dough is easy to whip up, and you refrigerate it before baking. Definitely roll it out thin. The dough may seem very crumbly, but no worries as it is all going to work out.

Makes approximately 80 cookies

1 cup canola oil
2 cups sugar
2 large eggs
3½ cups all-purpose flour
½ cup natural cocoa powder, such as Hershey's Baking Cocoa, plus more for rolling out the dough
½ teaspoon baking soda
½ teaspoon salt

NOTE: If the cookies are not crisp enough, bake for a minute or more longer, but be careful to not overbake. These chocolate cookies do not allow for the telltale "or until golden" rule.

1 In a large bowl, whisk together the oil, sugar, and eggs. In a separate bowl, whisk together the flour, cocoa, baking soda, and salt. Slowly stir the flour mixture into the oil mixture, stirring just enough to incorporate all the dry ingredients. Cover and refrigerate for 30 minutes.

2 Preheat the oven to 350°F. Line two baking sheets with parchment paper.

3 Divide the cookie dough into two equal batches and return one batch to the refrigerator. Lay a piece of the dough, dusted with a bit of cocoa, between two sheets of wax or parchment paper (the top layer prevents it from having the ghostly appearance that flour on top would cause) and work into a round. Roll out the dough to a thickness of ⅛ inch. Using a 1½-inch round cutter or juice glass, cut the cookies out and place them about 2 inches apart on the prepared baking sheets. Store the unbaked cookies in the refrigerator until ready to bake.

4 Bake the cookies for 7 minutes, until just firm—bake for 1 minute more if necessary, but no more than that (see Note). Repeat with the remaining cookies. Allow the cookies to cool completely on a wire rack. Store in an airtight container for up to 3 days.

GRAHAM CRACKERS

HANDS-ON TIME
20 minutes

TOTAL TIME
1 hour,
30 minutes

Whole wheat flour is what gives this cookie its texture and flavor, but you must roll it out carefully to avoid making great big cookies that one cannot bite into. These cookies would also work well as a crust and can be the base of other recipes, like Mallomars (page 63). Graham crackers are a lunch box staple because many parents assume grahams have less sugar than, say, a sandwich cookie. (They often do, though not a lot less sugar, but the balance of fiber to fat is a bit higher here than in commercial cookies.) *Makes 24 cookies*

2½ cups whole wheat flour

½ cup all-purpose flour, plus more for rolling out the dough

1 cup (packed) light brown sugar

½ teaspoon baking powder

½ teaspoon baking soda

½ teaspoon salt

¼ teaspoon cinnamon

½ cup (1 stick) cold salted butter, cut into small pieces

⅓ cup cold whole milk

NOTE: You want to make sure the dough is well chilled as you work it.

1 In a food processor, pulse the whole wheat and all-purpose flours, brown sugar, baking powder, baking soda, salt, and cinnamon 3 to 5 times, until just combined. Add the butter and pulse 15 to 20 times, or until the mixture resembles coarse meal. Add the milk all at once and process just until the mixture forms a ball, about 20 seconds. Shape the dough into a 1-inch-thick disk, wrap in plastic wrap, and refrigerate for 45 minutes to 1 hour.

2 Preheat the oven to 325°F. Line a baking sheet with parchment paper.

3 Unwrap the disk and place on a well-floured surface (see Note). With floured hands, shape the disk into a rectangle, then roll the dough out to a 9 × 12-inch rectangle.

4 Carefully transfer the dough rectangle to the prepared baking sheet. Trim the rectangle's edges to straight lines, removing excess scraps of dough. Score (but don't cut) the rectangle into four 3-inch-wide strips, then score each strip into six equal pieces. Use a fork to make holes in the top of each cookie several times.

5 Bake for 25 to 27 minutes, or until the cookies are set and begin to brown around the edges. Let cool completely on a wire rack. Once the cookies are cool, gently break them apart. Store in an airtight container for up to 3 days.

SORT-OF WINDMILLS

HANDS-ON TIME
20 minutes
TOTAL TIME
2 hours

Every household in which I grew up seemed to have a "dad dessert," that one thing everyone knew not to touch. My dad loved the Windmill cookie, fashioned in the Archway factory not far from my southwest Michigan town. He would dig into these cookies, a sort of dry gingersnap dotted with sliced almonds, while sitting in the backyard listening to the Tigers on his transistor radio and drinking black coffee. The cookie I once shunned is now a powerful source of memories and, like black coffee and the Tigers, is an acquired taste. *Makes approximately 100 cookies*

1 cup (2 sticks) salted butter, softened

1 cup (packed) light brown sugar

½ cup molasses

1 large egg

3½ cups all-purpose flour, plus more for shaping the dough

½ teaspoon baking powder

½ teaspoon baking soda

½ teaspoon cinnamon

½ teaspoon allspice

¼ cup (or about 2 ounces) sliced almonds, lightly toasted

NOTE: Our version doesn't have the shape of a windmill, which would likely require a mold or press, but the old-school flavor is spot-on. Be sure to slice the dough on the thin side or you will have giant cookies to contend with.

1 In the bowl of a heavy-duty stand mixer, cream the butter, brown sugar, and molasses together on medium speed until fluffy, about 1 minute. Add the egg and mix just until combined.

2 In a separate bowl, whisk together the flour, baking powder, baking soda, cinnamon, and allspice. With the mixer on low speed, slowly add the flour mixture to the butter mixture in batches, scraping down the bowl as needed. Continue to mix just until all the dry ingredients have been incorporated. Add the almonds and mix until evenly distributed. Cover the dough with plastic wrap and refrigerate for 15 minutes.

3 Remove the dough to a work surface and divide it into three batches. Place each batch of dough on an 18-inch strip of plastic wrap. With floured hands, shape each batch into a 10-inch log and wrap the plastic around the dough, twisting and folding the ends under. Freeze for 1 hour.

4 Preheat the oven to 350°F. Line a baking sheet with parchment paper.

5 Remove one batch of cookie dough from the refrigerator. Slice the log into ¼-inch rounds and set ½ inch apart on the prepared baking sheet. (I score the top of each cookie with an X to evoke something of a windmill.) Bake for 9 to 11 minutes, or just until the cookies are set. Let cool completely on a wire rack. Store in an airtight container for up to 3 days.

Eating a sandwich cookie is so pleasurable because it is really two foods: a cookie and its filling. The two-treats-in-one offers multiple textures and distinct flavors, plus a certain element of perpetual surprise— oh, frosting again! If you find the outside cookie shell cloying, or weirdly boring on the tongue, there's always chocolate cream or peanut butter or vanilla something or other waiting beneath to divert you, a feather pillow confection on a low-thread-count sheet.

Sandwich cookies also have their own associated rituals. For so many, an Oreo cookie must be consumed in two steps. First, the cookie is pulled apart and the icing of the bottom half is licked off, often slowly, perhaps for as long as a single commercial break. The second half of the cookie is then examined with a vague bit of hope that a smattering of frosting remains on it. Finally, both now-bare disks are wolfed down, and the process begins again. But then consider the E.L. Fudge cookies, the old Keebler cookie that is in essence a reverse Oreo, with a butter cookie exterior and a chocolate filling. My mother recalls these were best eaten as a whole cookie, because the chocolate enhanced the otherwise slightly bland exterior. (The version you will find on page 61 is not at all bland.)

So, to summarize: sometimes a sandwich cookie is a date with two desserts in one night; other times it's a monogamous relationship with a cookie of manifold qualities.

While Oreos may be the pinnacle of the sandwich cookie genus, they are in fact not its archetype. In 1908, a company called Sunshine gave the world the Hydrox cookie, a less sweet version of Nabisco's 1912 knockoff, the Oreo. With its extra sugar and slightly more dynamic texture, the Oreo was the first cookie to be specifically marketed to children, and it eventually buried its progenitor. Mallomars, another early sandwich-style cookie, were fashioned from marshmallows sandwiched between cookies. During the 1950s these became a mild obsession, particularly on the East Coast.

My personal favorite is the Nutter Butter, though it is to many a cookie that seems to exude testosterone. In *Rabbit at Rest*, the final book in John Updike's four-novel series, the main character extols this cookie's virtues, "delicious dipped into milk, first up to its peanut waist, and then the rest for a second bite."

A close second, however, may be the oatmeal creme pie, which of course is not remotely a pie, but a fantastic mix of sticky and sweet with the added veneer of health: it's cereal! I stay away from vending machines these days, but sometimes during late nights on Capitol Hill, I've been known to plunk down some George Washingtons for these bad boys.

VIENNA COOKIES

HANDS-ON TIME
20 minutes

TOTAL TIME
1 hour,
10 minutes

Vienna cookies, or fingers, as they are known commercially, are sort of mildly bland but definitely comforting, the macaroni and cheese of cookies, the sort of treat people hand out on long bus trips. The cookies were first marketed by Sunshine Biscuits in 1915, then acquired by Keebler in 1996, which of course went about perverting the original, as so many modern snack companies like to do, by introducing, for example, a lemon filling version. But the vanilla-flavored originals are what have provided succor to generations of Americans, who received them as children post chicken pox vaccine and as adults after giving blood. In 1994, thousands of Vienna cookies were sent to American troops, who took them to the border area between Rwanda and Zaire to share with scores of refugees.

Emulating the commercial version was not so easy. My first dough was wet and sticky, almost like brioche, and rendered something closer to a biscuit than a cookie. With the addition of more sugar and some vanilla, I found myself closer to the original, from the texture of the cookie to the slightly cloying cream. This recipe is for the sugar cookie fan in your life. It is important to score the cookies before putting them in the oven; otherwise they will puff up and look just awful. *Makes approximately 15 sandwich cookies*

for the cookie

- 1 cup granulated sugar
- ½ cup (1 stick) cold unsalted butter, cut into small pieces
- 1 large egg
- 1 teaspoon vanilla extract
- 2 cups all-purpose flour, plus more for rolling out the dough
- ¼ teaspoon baking soda
- ¼ teaspoon salt

1 Make the cookie dough: In a food processor, pulse the sugar and the ½ cup butter together 20 to 25 times, or until the mixture has the texture of wet sand. Add the egg and vanilla and pulse another 5 times.

2 In a separate bowl, whisk together the flour, baking soda, and salt, then add the flour mixture to the butter mixture in the food processor all at once. Pulse 10 to 15 times, or until the mixture resembles coarse meal. Pour onto a sheet of plastic wrap, shape into a 1-inch disk, wrap tightly, and refrigerate for 30 minutes.

3 Preheat the oven to 350°F. Line two baking sheets with parchment paper.

4 On a lightly floured surface, roll the unwrapped dough out to a thickness of ¼ inch, dusting the rolling pin and top of dough with

for the cream filling

2 tablespoons half-and-half

2 tablespoons unsalted butter, softened

1½ cups powdered sugar

flour. Using a 2½-inch round cutter, cut out the cookies and place them 1 inch apart on the prepared baking sheets. (Scraps of dough can be gathered and rerolled once.) Using the tip of a sharp knife, make several holes that go all the way through the dough in the top of each cookie.

5 Bake for 10 to 12 minutes or until the cookies are a pale golden brown. Let cool completely on a wire rack. Once cooled, turn half the cookies upside down.

6 Make the cream filling: In a small microwave-safe bowl, combine the half-and-half and the 2 tablespoons butter, and microwave on high for 30 seconds, or until the butter has melted. Measure the powdered sugar into a medium bowl and slowly add the butter mixture, stirring until smooth.

7 Scoop a small amount of the filling, about 1½ teaspoons, into the center of each upturned cookie. Top each with one of the plain cookies to make a sandwich. Store in an airtight container at room temperature for up to 3 days.

NUTTER BUTTERS

HANDS-ON TIME
50 minutes

TOTAL TIME
5 hours,
15 minutes

The Nutter Butter, first introduced in the 1960s, is a unique cookie among the sandwich variety because of its fun shape, which evokes an actual peanut. Decades ago, Nutter Butter Man, an animated peanut man whose attire and slightly twisted demeanor evoked Willy Wonka (Wilder, not Depp), serenaded a young boy on a swing with a commercial jingle, now lodged in my mind with Taylor Swift–song acuity. Recently, Nabisco has come up with disk-shaped versions of the cookie, enraging hardcore fans who have accused Nabisco of altering the recipe and rendering the cookies insufficiently sweet. So we'll stick to the original concept here. To make these guys at home, you can use the top half of a "bikini" cutter, but I fashioned a peanut-shaped cutter by bending an oval-shaped aluminum one into an eight, and it worked well.

You'll need an offset spatula to remove these cookies from the pan. The dough gets really soft and hard to work with once it is warm, so you should refrigerate it between batches. The real key here is cutting your cookies the right thickness—I've made some too-big ones, which tasted fine but were inauthentic in every other way, and some too-thin ones, which burned a bit and did not hold the frosting as well. *Makes approximately 22 sandwich cookies*

for the cookie

- ½ cup (1 stick) salted butter, softened
- ½ cup granulated sugar
- ½ cup (packed) light brown sugar
- ½ cup smooth peanut butter
- 2 large eggs
- 1 teaspoon vanilla extract
- 2½ cups bread flour (all-purpose will do), plus more for scoring the dough
- ¼ teaspoon baking soda
- ¼ teaspoon baking powder
- ¼ teaspoon salt

1 Make the cookie dough: In the bowl of a heavy-duty stand mixer, mix the ½ cup butter, the granulated and brown sugars, and the ½ cup peanut butter together on medium speed until just combined, about 30 seconds. Add the eggs one at a time, then add the vanilla, mixing just until each is incorporated.

2 In a separate bowl, whisk together the flour, baking soda, baking powder, and salt. With the mixer on low speed, slowly add the flour to the butter mixture in two or three batches, scraping down the sides of the bowl occasionally, mixing just until the dry ingredients are incorporated. (Mix in any remaining pockets of dry ingredients by hand.) Shape the dough into a round and slide it out onto a piece of plastic wrap. Wrap the dough tightly, shaping it into a 1-inch disk, and refrigerate it for 2 hours.

3 Preheat the oven to 350°F. Line two baking sheets with parchment paper.

RECIPE CONTINUES

for the filling

½ cup smooth peanut
    butter
¼ cup (½ stick) salted
    butter, softened
1 teaspoon vanilla extract
¾ cup powdered sugar
¼ teaspoon salt

**NOTE: You can use a knife
to frost them; a pastry
bag will be more precise.**

4 Unwrap the dough and place it between two pieces of wax paper
or parchment paper. Roll the dough out to a thickness of slightly less
than ¼ inch.

5 Using a bikini-shaped cookie cutter (any medium size will suffice),
cut out the cookies and place them 2 inches apart on the prepared
baking sheets. Use the tines of a fork to gently score the top of each
cookie into a crosshatch pattern. You should flour the fork first, or
else the dough will stick to the fork and the cookies may well break.
Bake for 11 to 13 minutes, or until the edges of the cookies just begin
to brown. Let cool completely on wire racks.

6 Make the filling: Turn half the cookies upside down. In the bowl of
a heavy-duty stand mixer, beat the ½ cup peanut butter and ¼ cup
butter together on medium speed. With the mixer on low speed, add
the vanilla, powdered sugar, and salt, and mix until smooth. Scoop
the filling into a disposable piping bag (see Note).

7 Pipe the peanut butter mixture around the perimeter of the
upturned cookies first, then fill in the outlined area, using about
1 teaspoon per cookie; you don't want the filling squishing out
the sides. (You can use a butter knife or offset spatula instead to
carefully spread it.) Top each frosted cookie with one of the plain
cookies to make a sandwich. Store in an airtight container at room
temperature for up to 3 days.

MINT MILANOS

The Milano cookie was always considered to be a more sophisticated treat than other childhood cookies because it had a European-sounding name, featured dark chocolate rather than milk, was oval instead of round in shape, and came in a bag. Indeed, Pepperidge Farm marketed its bagged cookies to adults, positioning them as the sort of thing one nibbled with after-dinner coffee served in a delicate cup rather than a "Welcome to Vegas" mug. As kids, we adored the mint version and would often eat an entire bag, paired with a bag of Pepperidge Farm Sausalitos, which were considered equally exotic because of their macadamia nuts and milk chocolate chips, which is an exciting diversion from the usual semisweet. Somehow, because the package had fewer cookies than other commercial types, it seemed okay to eat the entire bag in a sitting. (There are now, of course, several types of Milano, including orange ones and raspberry ones, which always seem mildly pandering.)

So did you buy that canoe pan I told you to get for your awesome Twinkies? It comes with a great cream infuser tube that you can use, after removing the end attachment, to press out the "logs" of dough that in baking will flatten out into perfect Milano shapes. Don't make them too big, unless you want supersized versions. *Makes approximately 20 sandwich cookies*

for the cookie

- ½ cup (1 stick) salted butter, softened
- 1 cup sugar
- 2 large eggs
- 1 teaspoon vanilla extract
- 2½ cups all-purpose flour
- 1 teaspoon baking powder

for the filling

- 1 cup (6 ounces) semisweet chocolate morsels
- ¼ cup (½ stick) salted butter, softened
- ½ teaspoon peppermint extract or ¼ teaspoon peppermint oil (see Note)

1 Preheat the oven to 315°F. Line two baking sheets with parchment paper.

2 Make the cookie dough: In the bowl of a heavy-duty stand mixer, cream the ½ cup butter and the sugar together at medium speed until light and fluffy, about 1 minute. With the mixer on medium-high speed, add the eggs, one at a time, and mix until the mixture is thickened and pale yellow in color, about 2 minutes. Add the vanilla and continue to mix until smooth, scraping down the sides of the bowl to incorporate.

3 In a medium bowl, whisk together the flour and baking powder. With the mixer on low speed, gradually add the flour mixture to the butter mixture in batches, mixing just until all the dry ingredients are incorporated.

RECIPE CONTINUES

NOTE: While peppermint extract is more easily available, I prefer peppermint oil, which gives a more intense mint flavor. If you do opt for mint oil instead, use half the amount indicated for the extract.

4 Transfer the dough to a piping bag and pipe 2 × 1-inch ovals, set about 1 inch apart, onto the prepared baking sheets. Bake the cookies for 22 to 25 minutes, or until golden brown. Allow the cookies to cool completely on a wire rack.

5 Make the filling: In a microwave-safe bowl, microwave the chocolate and the ¼ cup of butter on high for 1 minute, or until melted, stirring every 30 seconds. Stir in the peppermint extract and let sit for 5 minutes.

6 Transfer the chocolate mixture to a piping bag. Turn half the cookies upside down and pipe a thin layer of chocolate cream on top, about 1½ teaspoons for each. Top each with one of the plain cookies to make a sandwich. Store in an airtight container for up to 3 days.

OREOS

HANDS-ON TIME
30 minutes

TOTAL TIME
2 hours,
15 minutes

The mother of all sandwich cookies, the hundred-year-old Oreo remains an enormous crowd pleaser. What makes this cookie endearing are the qualities that first attracted snackers a century ago: the texture and the intricate exterior pattern. The ornamental markings were originally stamped out by brass rollers passing over sheets of chocolate dough; it has changed a bit over the years from a wreath-like pattern to its current design of boomerang-shaped triangles surrounding an X shape. The pattern has been endlessly discussed among design professionals, and the architecture critic Paul Goldberger once explained that it combines "homelike decoration with an American love of machine imagery, and in that combination lies a triumph of design."

For fans who plow through a bag late at night in front of infomercials for vegetable dicers, it is the Oreo's perfect ratio of cookie to cream that so entices them. While kids adore the Double Stuf version, an adult may view it as the cookie version of breast implants—a glorious concept taken to a point of excess. The Fauxreo was a difficult cookie to master; while it is not terribly hard to make a good chocolate wafer cookie, it is very hard to get the mildly salty chocolate flavor matched with the sort of squishy yet toothsome texture. My first version used vegetable oil, and the texture was far too dense. Butter came in, and I increased the amount of cocoa, which greatly improved the flavor. *Makes approximately 40 sandwich cookies*

for the cookie

1⅓ cups salted butter, softened

1 cup granulated sugar

2¾ cups all-purpose flour

1 cup natural cocoa powder, such as Hershey's Baking Cocoa, plus more for rolling out the dough

½ teaspoon baking soda

½ teaspoon salt

1 Make the cookie dough: In the bowl of a heavy-duty stand mixer, cream the 1⅓ cups butter and the granulated sugar together on medium speed until light and fluffy, about 1 minute. In a medium bowl, whisk together the flour, cocoa, baking soda, and salt. With the mixer on low speed, slowly add the flour mixture to the butter mixture in batches, beating just until all the dry ingredients are incorporated, scraping down the sides and the bottom of the bowl as needed. Divide the dough into two equal batches. Shape each into a 1-inch disk, cover in plastic wrap, and refrigerate for 30 minutes.

2 Preheat the oven to 325°F. Line two baking sheets with parchment paper.

RECIPE CONTINUES

for the filling

3 tablespoons half-and-half

2 tablespoons salted butter, softened

3 cups powdered sugar

NOTE: It can help to dust your wax paper (or parchment paper) with some cocoa to get things rolling.

3 Working with one batch of dough at a time, remove a disk from the refrigerator and place between two sheets of wax paper (see Note). Roll the dough out to a thickness of ⅛ inch. Using a 1½-inch round cutter, cut out the cookies and place them about ½ inch apart on the prepared baking sheet. Bake for 18 to 20 minutes, or until the cookies are set. Let the cookies cool completely on a wire rack. Repeat with the remaining cookie dough.

4 Make the filling: In a small saucepan, combine the half-and-half and the 2 tablespoons butter and stir constantly over medium heat until the butter melts and the mixture begins to bubble. Remove from the heat and let rest 5 minutes.

5 Turn half the cookies upside down. Put the powdered sugar in a medium bowl and slowly add the butter mixture, stirring by hand or with a mixer on low speed until smooth. Transfer the mixture to a piping bag and pipe a small amount, about 1 teaspoon, into the center of each upturned cookie. (You can also use an offset spatula instead of a piping bag.) Top each with one of the plain cookies to make a sandwich. Store in an airtight container at room temperature for up to 3 days.

VANILLA FUDGE SANDWICHES

HANDS-ON TIME
30 minutes

TOTAL TIME
50 minutes

The Oreo fan can be the worst sort of blind snack food loyalist, the sort of person who cannot see the joy in opposites, who claims the superiority of the classic cookie over all other indulgences and cannot be swayed. But the fan of the E.L. Keebler cookie (so named as in "everyone loves") is a cheekier snack lover, believing she has a secret, the cookie equivalent of the B-tracks from an underground garage band.

My friend Stephanie used to fight with her older sister over these elf-shaped cookies. The two concluded that the cookie part was superior to the filling and dealt with this issue by peeling the filling off "in one unbreakable brown Keebler elf silhouette" and tossing it in the sink. "Once the fudge was dispatched, my sister and I could enjoy stacks of those cookies by biting off Ernie's [aka the Keebler dude's] head, breaking the cookie along the etched-in lines on the surface, or seeing how many cookie flats we could shove in our mouths at once."

Our recipe provides a lighter, round-shaped version of this cookie, with a very satisfying chocolate center that no one would ever toss to the plumbing, and a sophisticated sugar cookie exterior that is easy to make and worthy of a dinner party.

Makes approximately 15 sandwich cookies

for the cookie

- 1 cup granulated sugar
- ½ cup (1 stick) cold salted butter, cut into small pieces
- 1 large egg
- 1 teaspoon vanilla extract
- 2 cups all-purpose flour, plus more for rolling out the dough
- ¼ teaspoon baking soda
- ¼ teaspoon salt

1 Make the cookie dough: In a food processor, pulse the sugar and butter together 20 to 25 times, or until the mixture has the texture of wet sand. Add the egg and vanilla and pulse another 5 times.

2 In a medium bowl, whisk together the flour, baking soda, and ¼ teaspoon of salt, then add to the butter mixture in the food processor all at once. Pulse 10 to 15 times, or until the mixture resembles coarse meal. Transfer the dough to a sheet of plastic wrap, shape into a 1-inch disk, wrap tightly, and refrigerate for 30 minutes.

3 Preheat the oven to 350°F. Line two baking sheets with parchment paper.

4 Roll the dough out to a thickness of ¼ inch, dusting the rolling pin and the top of dough with flour. Using a 2½-inch round cutter, cut out the cookies and place them 2 inches apart on the prepared

RECIPE CONTINUES

for the filling

¼ cup whole milk

2 tablespoons salted
   butter

1 cup powdered sugar

½ cup cocoa powder

¼ teaspoon salt

baking sheets. Using the tip of a sharp knife, poke several holes in the top of each cookie.

5 Bake for 10 to 12 minutes, or until light golden brown. Let cool completely on a wire rack.

6 Make the filling: In a small saucepan combine the milk and the butter and bring to a boil over medium-low heat, stirring constantly. Remove from the heat and let rest 5 minutes. Meanwhile, in a medium bowl, whisk together the powdered sugar, cocoa, and ¼ teaspoon of salt. Pour the milk mixture over the powdered sugar mixture, stirring constantly until smooth. Let cool to room temperature.

7 Turn half the cookies upside down. Transfer the filling to a piping bag and pipe a circle of icing, roughly a teaspoon, slightly smaller than the area of the cookie, in the middle of the upturned cookies. Top each with one of the plain cookies to make a sandwich. Store in an airtight container for up to 3 days.

MALLOMARS

These cookies have had a cult following since their inception in 1913. With their graham cracker crust, gooey marshmallow center, and the crackling of chocolate that covers the whole package, Mallomars are the something-for-everyone dessert. They are highly nostalgic for aging baby boomers from the East Coast, in particular those who used to eagerly await their arrival on store shelves, then plow through boxes of them while playing jump rope and jacks in the street. Mallomars were originally made in New Jersey, and their distribution was always heavily concentrated in the Northeast, even though they are now made in, of all places, Toronto. Interestingly, to prevent Mallomars from more or less melting in the summer, the factory that produces them stops in March and resumes in September, creating an off-season for the cookie that makes them as coveted and anticipated as Easter candy.

You can make your own Mallomars year-round. You just need a careful eye to get your marshmallow exactly soft enough to congeal on the cookie, but not so much that it becomes mush. *Makes approximately 40 cookies*

HANDS-ON TIME
40 minutes

TOTAL TIME
1 hour,
30 minutes

for the cookie

- 2 cups whole wheat flour
- ½ cup all-purpose flour
- 1 cup (packed) light brown sugar
- ½ teaspoon baking powder
- ½ teaspoon baking soda
- ½ teaspoon salt
- ½ cup (1 stick) cold salted butter, cut into small pieces
- ½ cup cold whole milk

1 Make the cookie dough: In a food processor, pulse the whole wheat and all-purpose flours, brown sugar, baking powder, baking soda, and salt together 3 to 5 times, until just combined. Add the ½ cup of cold butter pieces and pulse 15 to 20 times, or until the mixture resembles coarse meal. Add the milk all at once and process just until the mixture forms a ball, about 20 seconds.

2 Divide the dough into two equal batches and roll each between two sheets of parchment paper to a thickness of ¼ inch. Place the dough on a baking sheet, and refrigerate for 30 minutes to 1 hour.

3 Preheat the oven to 325°F. Line two baking sheets with parchment paper.

4 Working with one batch of dough at a time, cut circles using a 2-inch round cutter. Set cookies 1 inch apart on the prepared baking sheets. Bake for 10 to 11 minutes or until the cookies are just set. Let cool completely on wire racks.

RECIPE CONTINUES

for the filling

20 large marshmallows, halved crossways

for the chocolate coating

1 cup (2 sticks) salted butter
½ cup cold half-and-half
4 cups (24 ounces) semisweet chocolate morsels

5 Make the filling: Place half a marshmallow on top of each cookie, cut side down. Working in batches, place the marshmallow-topped cookies on a microwave-safe plate and microwave on high for 5 seconds, then check; continue to zap in 5-second intervals until the marshmallows are good and soft but not totally melted. Let the cookies sit at room temperature until the marshmallows cool to room temperature, about 10 minutes.

6 Make the chocolate coating: Cut the 1 cup of butter into 4 pieces and place in a medium heatproof bowl. In a small saucepan, bring 2 to 3 inches of water to a boil over medium heat. Turn the heat off and place the bowl of butter over the saucepan. Stir constantly until the butter melts. Add the cold half-and-half, and stir until combined. Pour the chocolate morsels into the melted butter, stirring constantly until the chocolate melts and the mixture is smooth.

7 Carefully dip each marshmallow-topped cookie into the chocolate, turning with a fork or offset spatula to cover all sides and allowing the excess chocolate to run off. Place the dipped cookies on a wire rack to set. Let set completely before storing. Store in an airtight container for up to 2 days.

OATMEAL CREME PIES

HANDS-ON TIME
25 minutes

TOTAL TIME
2 hours,
25 minutes

Oatmeal creme pies appear in every vending machine I come across in my professional life, and whenever I see one, I feel tempted. For many Americans, oatmeal creme pies are road-trip food, the sort one might find at a highway service stop, sandwiched somewhere between the Slim Jims and those cardboard-ish crackers with peanut butter.

This recipe takes the beloved Little Debbie classic and jazzes it up with some crazy cream. The cookie itself is not quite as crisp or as sweet as your average oatmeal cookie recipe—the cream is what fills out the flavor profile. *Makes approximately 30 sandwich cookies*

for the cookie

- 1½ cups vegetable oil
- ½ cup granulated sugar
- 1 cup (packed) dark brown sugar
- 2 large eggs, lightly beaten
- 2 teaspoons vanilla extract
- 2 cups all-purpose flour
- 1 teaspoon salt
- ¼ teaspoon baking powder
- 2 cups old-fashioned oats

for the filling

- 1 (7-ounce) container marshmallow fluff
- ⅓ cup salted butter
- 1 cup powdered sugar

NOTE: I found making these with a large melon scoop produced a more authentic and more evenly baked cookie. Do not use too much filling or you'll have a gooey mess.

1 Make the cookie dough: In the bowl of a heavy-duty stand mixer, blend the oil, granulated sugar, and brown sugar together at medium speed until thoroughly combined. Mix in the eggs, one at a time, until just combined. Stir in the vanilla. In a medium bowl, whisk together the flour, salt, baking powder, and oats. With the mixer on low speed, slowly stir the flour mixture into the oil mixture until the dry ingredients are just combined. Cover the bowl with plastic wrap and refrigerate for 2 hours, or up to 1 day.

2 Preheat the oven to 350°F. Line two baking sheets with parchment paper.

3 Place rounded tablespoons of the dough 3 inches apart on the prepared baking sheets. (Return any raw dough to the refrigerator until ready to bake.) Bake for 8 to 10 minutes, or just until set. (Overcooking will make for a crisp rather than a chewy cookie.) Place the baking sheets on wire racks to cool completely. Once cooled, turn half the cooled cookies upside down.

4 Make the filling: Using a hand mixer, beat the marshmallow fluff, butter, and powdered sugar together. Drop a small amount, about 1 teaspoon, of filling onto the center of each upturned cookie and top with one of the plain cookies to make a sandwich. Do not spread the fluff or press the cookies together; the weight of the top cookie will naturally spread the filling. Store in an airtight container in the refrigerator for up to 3 days.

In the panoply of nostalgic junk foods, snack cakes are the ne plus ultra, the measure by which any and all other treats must be judged. One's passion, and subsequent elegy, is usually driven by geography and generation—a Long Island baby boomer would have lived off Yodels and Devil Dogs, made by Drake's, while a midwesterner would have been drawn to products made by Hostess, like its cream-filled cupcakes or the infamous Twinkie, that indestructible pale squish of sponge cake filled with cloying cream.

While many snack cakes now enjoy broad distribution, some remain limited to certain regions of the country, and a few, like the Moon-Pie, are really hard to find anywhere outside of a state or two. Upon finding herself back in familiar territory, a traveler might find herself racing to the nearest 7-Eleven in search of the snack cake of her youth.

Snack cake memories tend to be place- and product-specific. Some people have fond and vivid memories of curling up with a good book and a Ring Ding, while others associate the lazy pleasures of a middle school Friday afternoon with the peanut butter–laden Funny Bones.

Those memories are so enduring, and so classically American, that they've been celebrated in films, television shows, and the visual arts. In a famous scene in *Ghostbusters*, Dr. Egon Spengler uses a Twinkie to help explain the "normal amount of psychokinetic energy in the New York area." A 1992 episode of *Seinfeld* was partially dedicated to the examination of the finer qualities of a Drake's cake.

Just as everyone has their favorite snack cake, everyone has a preferred method of eating them. Some like to peel the frosting off a Hostess Cup Cake, excavate the creamy center with the tongue, and then pop the remaining bits of chocolate cake into the mouth. A Suzy Q would often leak cream out of its sides and could be licked like an ice cream cone before a bite of the cake was ever attempted.

Some snack cakes were deconstructed, then eaten, because their flavors and textures were best enjoyed separately; others were more pleasurable comingled. A Ho Ho would occasionally leave a bit of greasy residue on the plastic wrapper or paper insert, which a child would certainly scrape away with a fingernail and quickly lick off; an adult would have greater issues of propriety to consider before indulging in this final act.

Snack cakes can be labor intensive, and the recipes work best when you invest in a few small pieces of equipment, such as an infuser for cream centers and, in some cases, a special pan. Your frosting will no doubt be richer and fuller of chocolate flavor than you remember, and your creams less stable. But the authenticity of the pleasure is guaranteed.

TWINKIES

The Twinkie is, of course, the ultimate snack cake, by virtue of its iconic shape, indestructible composition, and evocative name. When you refer to someone unserious as a "Twinkie," the snack cake is instantly anthropomorphized as a porous, insubstantial thing whose probing rewards only sugary goo. And yet the Twinkie also evokes its fancy French cousin, the éclair, or its working-class cousin, the long john donut. I outgrew the Twinkie early in my snacking life, preferring the clarion call of chocolate treats and fruit-filled offerings. But as I grew up, I had a greater appreciation for the sponge cake concept because it is light and so deliciously absorbs macerated fruit juices and caramel-based sauces.

Your sponge cake, absent chemical stabilizers, will also take on this sophisticated quality while maintaining that sweet center surprise. It took me a few tries to get the cream quite stable. A buttercream version was absorbed by the cake, destroying its Twinkie integrity. Marshmallow fluff solved the problem. You may construct individual Twinkie molds from aluminum foil, which is difficult and messy, or make these in cupcake pans, which will compromise their authenticity, or spring for a canoe pan with its cream injector if you're truly obsessed. *Makes 14 cakes*

for the cake

4 large eggs
½ cup (1 stick) salted butter, softened
1½ cups granulated sugar
2 teaspoons vanilla extract
⅓ cup whole milk
2 cups all-purpose flour
½ teaspoon baking powder
¼ teaspoon salt

for the filling

½ cup marshmallow fluff
½ cup powdered sugar
5 tablespoons salted butter, softened

1 Preheat the oven to 325°F. Use unsalted butter or nonstick cooking spray to lightly grease your muffin pan or canoe pan.

2 Make the cake batter: Separate the eggs into two separate bowls, yolks in one and whites in the other. In a heavy-duty stand mixer, beat the egg whites on high speed until stiff peaks form, about 3 minutes. Transfer the egg whites to a clean bowl.

3 In a heavy-duty stand mixer, cream the butter and granulated sugar together until light and fluffy, about three minutes. Add the egg yolks and continue to beat until the mixture is thick, creamy, and pale yellow, about 4 minutes. Add the vanilla extract and milk, and beat for an additional 5 seconds. Gently stir a third of the egg whites into the mixture by hand.

RECIPE CONTINUES

4 In a separate medium bowl, whisk together the flour, baking powder, and salt. Add the remaining egg whites to the wet mixture, folding them in by hand until just incorporated. Add the flour mixture to the wet mixture, and gently combine the two mixtures just until all the dry ingredients are incorporated.

5 Spoon the batter into the canoe or muffin pans, filling each cup with ¼ cup of batter. Bake for 20 to 22 minutes, or until the cakes are lightly golden and spring back when lightly touched. Let cool completely on a wire rack.

6 Make the filling: In a clean bowl and using an electric hand or stand mixer, beat the marshmallow fluff, powdered sugar, and the 5 tablespoons butter until combined and fluffy, about 1 minute.

7 Turn each cake over so the flat side is facing up. Using the handle of a small fork or spoon, gently make three holes in the flat side of each cake, spaced evenly apart and not too large. (If using a muffin tin, make just one hole in the center of each cake.) Gently rotate the utensil in each hole to create a small cavity at each opening. Transfer the filling to a piping bag and fill each opening with just enough marshmallow mixture to fill each hole. Serve immediately.

DONUT HOLES

This treat, misspelled and oddly placed on the shelf, is one of life's greatest inventions, the chicken nugget of the breakfast table. Any foodstuff that can fit in its entirety into your mouth in a single bite is a wonderful thing. The donut hole is like the donut distilled, amplified, concentrated—the donut in extremis, though Lilliputian, not so much the donut hole as the donut soul.

Makes approximately 45 donut holes

HANDS-ON TIME
20 minutes

TOTAL TIME
45 minutes

for the donut

- 2½ cups all-purpose flour
- ¾ cup granulated sugar
- ¾ teaspoon baking powder
- ¼ teaspoon salt
- ½ cup (1 stick) cold salted butter, cut into small pieces
- 1 large egg
- 1 cup whole milk
- Vegetable oil for frying (optional)

for the glaze

- 2 cups powdered sugar
- ¼ cup whole milk

NOTE: A donut hole pan can be purchased at many baking and cooking retailers online.

NOTE: You can bake or fry the donut holes. I prefer to bake them, which I find less messy and plenty delicious, and authentic without the unpleasant grease.

1 Make the donut hole: In a medium bowl, whisk together the flour, granulated sugar, baking powder, and salt. Using a pastry cutter, cut the butter into the flour until the butter pieces are no bigger than small peas. In a separate bowl, whisk together the egg and the 1 cup of milk, and stir the egg mixture into the flour mixture by hand.

2 If baking the donut holes: Preheat the oven to 425°F. Scoop heaping tablespoons of the dough into a greased donut hole pan (see Note) and bake for 7 to 9 minutes, or until the holes are puffed and just beginning to brown around the edges. Let cool in the pan for 10 minutes, then move to step 4.

3 If frying the donut holes: In a large uncovered Dutch oven, heat 2 inches of vegetable oil over medium-high heat to 350°F, or until a drop of dough sizzles and floats on contact with the oil. Drop tablespoons of the batter into the oil in batches, cooking each batch for 2 minutes, turning halfway through cooking so that all sides are evenly browned. Remove with a slotted spoon or wire mesh sieve to a paper towel–lined plate to drain. Cool for 10 minutes.

4 Place a lightly greased wire rack over a rimmed baking sheet to hold the donut holes when glazed.

5 Make the glaze: In a medium bowl, combine the powdered sugar and the ¼ cup milk, stirring until smooth. Working in batches, drop the donut holes into the glaze, turning each with a fork until evenly coated. Place the glazed donut holes on the greased wire rack to set, about 15 minutes. Serve immediately.

STAR CRUNCH

HANDS-ON TIME
20 minutes

TOTAL TIME
2 hours,
20 minutes

I confess this is not a snack food with which I had much experience, but many readers clamored for the Little Debbie confection they had nibbled on in the Northeast. It is essentially chocolate cereal as a cookie, so you have to be okay with that. This recipe works well either with dark chocolate, for a bit of a sophisticated city-girl take, or with milk chocolate, for the hey-I'm-just-chillin'-in-front-of-the-afterschool-special vibe. There is absolutely no skill needed to make these—you do need fingers for the microwave—and they would make a great quick bake sale item.

Makes approximately 20 cookies

30 caramels (about
   2 cups)
¾ cup heavy cream
1¼ cups (7.5 ounces)
   semisweet chocolate
   chips
1 teaspoon vanilla extract
1 tablespoon molasses
¼ teaspoon salt
5 cups crisp puffed rice
   cereal, such as Rice
   Krispies

1 In a microwave-safe bowl, combine the caramels with ¼ cup of the cream and microwave for 1 minute, or until melted and smooth, stirring every 30 seconds.

2 In a separate microwave-safe bowl, combine the chocolate and the remaining ½ cup of cream and microwave for 1 to 1½ minutes, or until the chocolate has melted, stirring every 30 seconds. Combine the caramel and chocolate mixtures and stir in the vanilla, molasses, and salt.

3 Place the cereal in a large bowl and pour the chocolate-caramel mixture over the cereal. Using a large rubber spatula, stir until thoroughly combined.

4 Line a baking sheet with wax paper.

5 Scoop 2-inch-wide mounds of the cereal mixture onto the baking sheet and flatten slightly with the back of a wooden spoon. Let sit for 2 hours, or until the chocolate is set. Store in an airtight container for up to 2 days.

BUTTERSCOTCH KRIMPETS

HANDS-ON TIME
40 minutes

TOTAL TIME
2 hours

Butterscotch Krimpets were a favorite among those who grew up with Tastykakes in the Northeast, but newcomers were also turned on by the deep butterscotch yumminess against an airy cake base, made fluffy in our recipe by whipping the egg whites, which helps give the cake a lift.

The recipe procedure is a sophisticated one for a sort of low-down cake, but, babies, it's worth it. You can make these cakes in a muffin pan, but for authenticity, make the whole recipe in a cake pan and then cut out individual squares. *Makes twelve 3-inch-square cake slices*

for the cake

4 large eggs
½ cup (1 stick) salted butter, softened
1½ cups granulated sugar
2 teaspoons vanilla extract
⅓ cup whole milk
2 cups all-purpose flour
½ teaspoon baking powder
¼ teaspoon salt

for the icing

1½ cups (3 sticks) unsalted butter
2½ cups powdered sugar
½ teaspoon salt

1 Preheat the oven to 325°F. Lightly grease and line a 9 × 13-inch baking sheet with parchment paper, leaving a 2-inch overhang of paper on both sides of the pan.

2 Make the cake batter: Separate the eggs into two separate bowls, yolks in one and whites in the other. In a heavy-duty stand mixer, beat the egg whites on high speed until stiff peaks form, about 3 minutes. Transfer the egg whites to a clean bowl.

3 In a heavy-duty stand mixer, cream the ½ cup butter and the granulated sugar together until light and fluffy, about 1 minute. Add the egg yolks and continue to beat until the mixture is thick, creamy, and pale yellow, about 4 minutes. Add the vanilla and milk and beat for an additional 5 seconds. Gently fold a third of the egg whites into the egg yolk mixture by hand.

4 In a separate bowl, whisk together the flour, baking powder, and salt. Add the remaining egg whites to the egg yolk mixture and fold in by hand until just combined. Add the flour mixture with the mixer on low speed and continue to gently combine the ingredients just until all the dry ingredients are incorporated.

5 Spoon the batter into the prepared baking sheet. Bake for 25 to 28 minutes, or until the cake is set and lightly golden. Let cool completely on a wire rack.

6 Make the icing: In a small saucepan placed over medium heat, melt the 1½ cups butter. Immediately turn the heat down to medium-low, and continue to cook the melted butter until it browns to the color of honey, about 15 minutes (see Note). Remove the pan from the heat and let the butter rest for 5 minutes.

7 Slowly pour the melted butter into a medium bowl, taking care to keep the dark butter solids separate, to be discarded. Let this clarified butter cool to room temperature.

8 Using a stand mixer or an electric hand mixer, beat the powdered sugar, browned butter, and salt together on medium speed until smooth and fluffy.

9 Use the parchment overhang to remove the cake from the baking pan and place it on a cutting board. Using a rubber or offset spatula, spread the frosting evenly over the cake. Cut the frosted cake into 3-inch squares. Serve immediately.

DRAKE'S COFFEE CAKES

HANDS-ON TIME
25 minutes

TOTAL TIME
1 hour,
5 minutes

The Drake's coffee cake, another Northeast classic, was immortalized in a *Seinfeld* episode in which the gang trade favors for this much beloved cinnamon-scented doozy. Good coffee cake is one of the most American of all desserts, and it's the most versatile. It is a widely accepted breakfast item, dotting the breakfast buffets of scores of cheap hotels and motels, placed somewhere between the sad scrambled egg dish and a basket of overly ripe Red Delicious apples.
Makes approximately 24 mini coffee cakes

for the streusel topping

¾ cup all-purpose flour, plus more for the tin

1½ cups (packed) brown sugar

1 teaspoon salt

⅓ cup salted butter, melted, plus more for the tin

for the cake

¾ cup (1½ sticks) salted butter, softened

1½ cups granulated sugar

3 large eggs

2 teaspoons vanilla extract

3 cups all-purpose flour

¼ teaspoon baking powder

½ teaspoon salt

1 cup sour cream

NOTE: Don't overload the streusel topping: when it melts, it expands, and it will be a mouthful of topping for a taste of cake.

1 Make the streusel topping: In a medium bowl, combine the ¾ cup flour, the brown sugar, and the salt . Pour the ⅓ cup of melted butter over the top and stir to combine. Set aside.

2 Preheat the oven to 350°F. Generously butter and flour a muffin tin.

3 Make the cake batter: In a heavy-duty stand mixer, cream the ¾ cup of butter and the granulated sugar on medium speed just until light and fluffy, about 1 minute. Add the eggs, one at a time, mixing well after each, until the mixture is thick and creamy, about 3 minutes. Add the vanilla and mix for 5 seconds more.

4 In a separate bowl, whisk together the flour, baking powder, and salt. With the mixer on low speed, add a third of the flour mixture to the butter mixture, then half of the sour cream. Repeat again with the second third of the flour mixture and the second half of the sour cream. End by folding in the last third of the flour by hand.

5 Fill each cup of the muffin tin about half full of cake batter. Top each cake with a full tablespoon of streusel. Bake for 18 to 20 minutes, or until a toothpick inserted in the middle comes out with just a few crumbs attached.

6 Cool the cakes, still in the pan, on a wire rack for 10 minutes, then carefully remove them from the pan. Serve warm or at room temperature. Store in an airtight container at room temperature for up to 2 days.

ZEBRA CAKES

HANDS-ON TIME
35 minutes

TOTAL TIME
2 hours,
35 minutes

The Zebra Cake is one of life's great snack cakes, largely because it transforms the birthday or wedding cake concept into bite-size portions, giving you a special-occasion cake without the wait. In suburban Houston, my nephew Dustin said that Zebra Cakes were the postgame snack of choice for most soccer families when he was growing up. "You would think that after playing soccer in one-hundred-degree heat with raging humidity of Houston, the last thing you would want would be a piece of cake. False. Zebra Cakes seemed to taste even better then."

These cakes are slightly time consuming but really a lot of fun to make. Once you've made the cake base—and you definitely needed the full baking time; for some reason, this is a slow-baking cake—put it in the refrigerator, my new favorite technique for firming up a cake before cutting it into layers. After slicing the cake into two layers, I frost the top of the bottom layer, carefully slide the top layer back into place, and refrigerate the cake again. I then make the glaze—the yield here is plentiful, and you want to glaze the entire cake, making sure to get plenty on the sides. *Makes one 9 × 13-inch cake*

for the cake

4 large eggs
½ cup (1 stick) salted butter, softened
1½ cups granulated sugar
2 teaspoons vanilla extract
⅓ cup whole milk
2 cups all-purpose flour
½ teaspoon baking powder
¼ teaspoon salt

for the filling

2 cups marshmallow fluff
⅔ cup salted butter, softened
1 cup powdered sugar

1 Preheat the oven to 325°F. Lightly grease a 9 × 13-inch cake pan and line it with parchment paper, leaving a 2-inch overhang on both sides of the pan.

2 Make the cake batter: Separate the eggs into two bowls, yolks in one and whites in the other. In a heavy-duty stand mixer, beat the egg whites on high speed until stiff peaks form, about 3 minutes. Transfer the beaten egg whites into a clean bowl.

3 In a heavy-duty stand mixer, cream the ½ cup of butter and the granulated sugar together until light and fluffy, about 1 minute. Add the egg yolks and continue to beat until the mixture is thick, creamy, and pale yellow, about 4 minutes. Add the vanilla and milk, and beat for an additional 5 seconds. By hand, gently stir a third of the egg whites into the butter mixture.

4 In a separate bowl, whisk together the flour, baking powder, and salt. By hand, fold the remaining egg whites into the butter mixture

RECIPE CONTINUES

for the glazes

⅓ cup half-and-half
3 cups powdered sugar
¼ cup (1.5 ounces)
   semisweet chocolate
   morsels

NOTE: Regarding the striped frosting: I like to use a spoon to drizzle the zebra chocolate stripes. Alternatively, you can cut the cake into slices first, then dip the slices in the frosting and stripe them one by one for verisimilitude (but that will be more work/mess).

until just combined. Add the flour mixture to the butter mixture and continue to gently by hand and combine just until all the dry ingredients are incorporated.

5 Spoon the batter into the pan. Bake for 25 to 28 minutes, or until the cake is set and lightly golden. Let cool on a wire rack for 10 minutes, then remove the cake from the pan and let cool completely.

6 Make the filling: Using a stand mixer or an electric hand mixer, beat the marshmallow fluff, the ⅔ cup of butter, and the 1 cup of powdered sugar together until combined and fluffy, about 1 minute.

7 Using a long serrated bread knife, slice the cake into 2 equal layers. Spread the marshmallow filling evenly over the top of one cake layer, then carefully top with the remaining layer. Refrigerate the cake for 30 minutes.

8 Make the two glazes: For the white glaze, in a medium bowl, combine all but 1 tablespoon of the half-and-half and all of the 3 cups of powdered sugar, whisking until smooth. For the "stripe" glaze, in a small glass bowl, microwave the chocolate morsels for 1 minute on high, stirring every 30 seconds, until melted and smooth. Add ¼ cup of the white glaze and the remaining 1 tablespoon of the half-and-half to the melted chocolate, and stir until smooth. Transfer the chocolate glaze to a piping bag.

9 Slowly pour the white glaze over the top of the cake, using an offset spatula to smooth the glaze over the top and down the sides of the entire cake. Allow the cake to set for 1 hour, then use a spoon to drizzle the top of the chilled cake with the chocolate glaze in a striped pattern (see Note). Let the cake rest uncovered at room temperature until set, about 1 hour more. Store the cake in an airtight container for up to 2 days.

DEVIL DOGS

The Devil Dog in some ways presaged the cupcake craze by decades, with its somewhat dry devil's food chocolaty exterior and its overly sweet cream center. The treats are presented in a sort of hot dog shape, with a devil's food bun and cream filling instead of a frank. *Makes approximately 12 sandwich cookies*

HANDS-ON TIME
30 minutes

TOTAL TIME
1 hour

for the cookie

½ cup (1 stick) salted butter, softened
1 cup granulated sugar
2 large eggs
1 teaspoon vanilla extract
2 cups all-purpose flour
⅓ cup natural cocoa powder, such as Hershey's Baking Cocoa
1 teaspoon baking soda
½ teaspoon salt
1 cup whole milk

for the filling

1 cup heavy whipping cream
3 tablespoons powdered sugar
1 teaspoon vanilla extract

NOTE: Compared with the commercial Devil Dog, our version is far lighter and less sweet, and although the cream isn't stable, it's also not cloying. We make our dogs in rounds, but if you crave authenticity, you can get a doggier shape by using your canoe pan or a mold.

1 Preheat the oven to 400°F. Line two baking sheets with parchment paper.

2 Make the cookie dough: In a heavy-duty stand mixer, cream the butter and the granulated sugar together on medium speed until light and fluffy, about 1 minute. Add the eggs one at a time, mixing well after each addition. Add one teaspoon of the vanilla and mix for an additional 5 seconds.

3 In a medium bowl, whisk together the flour, cocoa, baking soda, and salt. With the mixer on low speed, gradually add the flour mixture to the butter mixture in batches alternating with the milk, beginning and ending with the flour, and beating after each addition until just blended.

4 Set ¼-cup scoops of batter spaced 3 inches apart on the prepared baking sheets. Bake for 9 minutes, or just until the cookies are set. (If you are using multiple pans, bake one pan at a time.) Cool the cookies on the pans for 10 minutes, then remove them to a wire rack to cool completely.

5 Make the filling: Using a stand mixer or an electric hand mixer, beat the whipping cream, powdered sugar, and the 1 teaspoon of vanilla on high for 1 minute, or until stiff peaks form.

6 Just prior to serving, turn half the cookies upside down. Top the upturned cookies with the whipped cream, about 3 tablespoons on each. Cover each with one of the plain cookies to make a sandwich.

SNACK CAKES |

HONEY BUNS

HANDS-ON TIME
35 minutes
TOTAL TIME
**1 hour,
30 minutes**

For many years during my midwestern upbringing, the Honey Bun was not so much a snack as my actual lunch. Large cinnamon rolls doused in cloying vanilla frosting, these buns were so substantial that one for breakfast would easily get me through until French class, where I would generally be three chapters behind everyone else. After class, I would eagerly remove another bun from its cellophane wrapper, the frosting immediately covering my fingers, and lean against a wall to gossip with friends. The top of these buns was so wide, it could also serve as a canvas: I once carved an obscenity in the cream, dropped it on my philandering soon-to-be ex-boyfriend's doorstep, rang the bell, and ran. Snack foods, as you can see, did little to enhance my emotional growth.

To get this recipe right, I turned to the home baker's dirty secret, laminated dough, so called because of its alternating layers of butter and dough. It's what's used in croissants and Danish pastry, members of the glorious baking family called *viennoiserie*. You really can't make it easily from scratch, but thankfully it's available in mixes with superfast-rising yeast. This kind of laminated dough is what Gail the cookie lady calls "turbocharged bread, often enriched with eggs or oil to make it tastier." Generally with yeasted products, the yeast needs time to activate and begin producing gas to make the bread rise and become light and fluffy. A laminated dough has a bit of yeast in it, but then, like puff pastry, it has copious amounts of butter slathered all over it and is rolled and turned several times to produce gorgeous flaky layers. This thing is so danged delicious, people will actually get mad at you when you serve it.
Makes 15 honey buns

for the honey glaze (makes about 2 cups)

1 cup (2 sticks) salted butter, melted
1 cup honey
½ cup (packed) light brown sugar
½ teaspoon salt

1 Make the honey glaze: In a medium bowl, stir the melted butter, honey, brown sugar, and salt together and set aside. Pour ¾ cup of the glaze into the bottom of a lightly greased 9 × 13-inch pan. Set the pan aside; reserve the remaining glaze.

2 Make the buns: In a large bowl, whisk together the flour mixture and yeast packet from the hot roll mix. In a cup, stir together the egg and the 2 tablespoons of melted butter. Then, using a fork or a wooden spoon, stir the egg mixture into the flour mixture. Stir in 1 cup of hot water, mixing until just combined.

RECIPE CONTINUES

for the buns

All-purpose flour, for rolling out the dough

1 (16-ounce) box hot roll mix (Pillsbury makes a great one)

1 large egg

2 tablespoons salted butter, melted

for the drizzle glaze

1 cup powdered sugar

2 tablespoons whole milk

NOTE: If some of the honey stuff gathers at the edge of the pan, scoop it up and re-drizzle the top with it.

3 Place the dough on a well-floured surface and knead for 5 minutes. Cover with a warm, damp cloth and let rest for 5 minutes. The dough should look smooth and be just slightly tacky to the touch, and it will have about doubled in size.

4 Roll the dough out into a 9 × 15-inch rectangle, with the long side running parallel to the counter edge. Brush ¾ cup of the remaining honey glaze over the top and roll the dough away from you into a log. Slice the rolled dough into 1-inch-thick rolls. Set the sliced rolls on their side touching one another into the prepared pan, and cover loosely with plastic wrap. Place in a warm (80°F) location for 30 minutes, or until the rolls have nearly doubled in size.

5 Preheat the oven to 350°F. Brush the buns with half of the remaining honey glaze, about ¼ cup. Bake for 20 to 22 minutes, or until golden brown. Remove the pan from the oven and immediately brush the buns with the remaining ¼ cup of honey glaze (see Note). (If the glaze has set, heat for 20 seconds in the microwave, then stir until smooth.) Let the buns cool in the pan on a wire rack until they are just barely warm.

6 Make the drizzle glaze: In a small bowl, stir together the powdered sugar and milk for the drizzle. Dip the tines of a fork into the glaze, then drizzle it over the mostly cooled buns. Serve warm or at room temperature. Store in an airtight container for up to 2 days.

MOONPIES

MoonPies are one of our nation's few treats that remain largely a regional item. They were born in Chattanooga, as part of a larger company that made its own versions of Fig Newton–style cookies, imitation Nilla Wafers, and other treats available in the South. This snack was conceived in 1917 at the request of miners who said they needed something substantial—as big as a moon, the lore goes—to fill their tummies as they went about their arduous work. The cookie was indeed dense, compressed almost like sawdust, but as with so many chocolate-coated treats, the thrill was breaking through the hard shell to the spongy marshmallow inside and having the cookie give little resistance in the journey. The snacks, long associated with miners, became a cult hit of the South and inspired the 1950s country song "Give Me an RC and a MoonPie," celebrating two local hits of sugar. While MoonPies—which now come in banana flavor and other varieties beyond the classic chocolate—are distributed around the United States, they remain distinctly associated with the South.

You could use the same base cookie as the Mallomar for a more authentic MoonPie texture, but I prefer this dough: its sweetened condensed milk gives it a less substantial and less cardboardy texture, with a bit more flavor than the original.

Makes approximately 20 sandwich cookies

HANDS-ON TIME
45 minutes

TOTAL TIME
2 hours

for the cookie

- ½ cup (1 stick) unsalted butter, softened
- 1 cup granulated sugar
- 1 large egg
- 1 cup sweetened condensed milk
- 1 teaspoon vanilla extract
- 2 cups all-purpose flour
- ¾ teaspoon salt
- ½ cup unsweetened cocoa powder
- 1½ teaspoons baking soda
- ½ teaspoon baking powder

1 Preheat the oven to 400°F. Line two baking sheets with parchment paper: one for the baking of the cookies, one for the final dipped cookie preparation.

2 Make the cookie dough: In the bowl of a standing mixer, cream the ½ cup butter and the granulated sugar together on high speed until fluffy, about 3 minutes. Add in the egg, condensed milk, and vanilla.

3 In a separate bowl, whisk together the flour, salt, cocoa, baking soda, and baking powder. Fold the flour mixture into the milk mixture by hand just until all the ingredients are combined.

RECIPE CONTINUES

for the filling
12 jumbo marshmallows

for the glaze
1 cup (2 sticks) unsalted
  butter
1 cup cocoa powder
2 cups powdered sugar

NOTE: Be careful when melting the marshmallow that you get it soft enough to squish, but not so soft that it runs.

4 With a small cookie scoop or tablespoon, place blobs of dough roughly 3 inches apart on one of the prepared baking sheets. Bake 5 to 8 minutes, checking halfway. The finished cookies should be firm, but not crisp. Remove and let cool for 1 hour.

5 Make the filling: Slice each marshmallow into three equal disks. Top half the cookies with a marshmallow disk. Working in batches, place the marshmallow-topped cookies on a microwave-safe plate and microwave on high for a few seconds at a time, checking often, so the marshmallows get nice and sticky but not totally melted (see Note). Top the marshmallow-covered cookies with the remaining plain cookies, but do not press. Let the cookies sit at room temperature until the marshmallows cool to room temperature, about 30 minutes.

6 Make the glaze: In a microwave-safe bowl, microwave the 2 sticks of butter on high heat for 1 minute. Let cool 5 minutes. Stir the cocoa and powdered sugar into the melted butter until smooth.

7 Dip each cookie sandwich into the chocolate, coating all sides and letting the excess chocolate drip back into the bowl. Place the cookies on the other baking sheet to set, about 1 hour. Store in an airtight container at room temperature for up to 3 days.

HOSTESS CUP CAKES

HANDS-ON TIME
40 minutes

TOTAL TIME
1 hour,
30 minutes

The Hostess Cup Cake is second perhaps only to the Twinkie and is best known for its oddly alluring plastic-like chocolate frosting with white squiggles, which spreads across the top like a bedspread, hiding the chocolate crumb cake and creamy center beneath. The frosting is often eaten as its own rightful snack, peeled away, considered, nibbled on, perhaps put back, maybe set to rest on a desk while you make your way into the cake. Or, if you do as one kid at my third grade lunch table preferred, you can dip it into your milk with the dim hope that somehow it will transform into chocolate milk. (Of course, this does not work—the frosting bit will instead float and bob, like a lonely chocolate seahorse, in the paper milk carton.)

This recipe is close to any standard cupcake version you may have on hand, but it is infused with cream and then dipped in chocolate, which sounds like a lot of work, but it all goes pretty quickly. *Makes 18 cupcakes*

for the cupcakes

1 cup (2 sticks) salted butter, softened
2 cups granulated sugar
2 large eggs
1 cup natural cocoa powder, such as Hershey's Baking Cocoa
2½ cups all-purpose flour
1 teaspoon baking soda
¼ teaspoon salt
½ cup whole milk

for the filling

1 cup marshmallow fluff
⅓ cup salted butter, softened
½ cup powdered sugar

1 Preheat the oven to 350°F. Line a 6- and 12-muffin tin with paper liners.

2 Make the cupcake batter: In the bowl of a heavy-duty stand mixer, cream the 2 sticks of butter and the granulated sugar together at medium speed just until light and fluffy, about 1 minute. Add the eggs, one at a time, and mix just until combined. In a measuring cup, stir ½ cup of hot water and the cocoa together until smooth. Add the cocoa mixture to the butter mixture and mix on low speed for an additional 10 seconds.

3 In a medium bowl, whisk together the flour, baking soda, and salt. With the mixer on low speed, gradually add the flour mixture to the butter mixture in batches alternating with the milk, beginning and ending with the flour and beating after each addition until the ingredients are just blended.

4 Fill each prepared muffin cup half full with chocolate batter. Bake for 22 to 25 minutes, or until a toothpick inserted in the middle comes out clean. Let cool completely on a wire rack.

RECIPE CONTINUES

for the frosting

⅓ cup heavy cream

1 cup (8 ounces) bittersweet chocolate morsels

1½ tablespoons salted butter, softened

for the frosting decoration (optional)

¼ cup (½ stick) unsalted butter, softened

½ cup powdered sugar

5 Make the filling: Using a clean bowl and a stand mixer or an electric hand mixer, beat the marshmallow fluff, the ⅓ cup of butter, and the ⅓ cup of powdered sugar together until combined and fluffy, about 1 minute. Using the handle of a small fork or spoon, make a hole in the top center of each cake. Gently rotate the utensil in each hole to create a small cavity at each opening. Transfer the filling to a piping bag and pipe in just enough marshmallow mixture to fill each hole. As with the Twinkie, you want a firm grasp on your cupcake as you infuse it with the filling, so as not to allow it to explode; once you feel it growing in size, stop infusing. Use a wet fingertip or the back of a spoon to tamp down any marshmallow peaks, ensuring that the filling is even with the top of the cupcake.

6 Make the frosting: In a small saucepan, heat the cream over medium heat just until bubbles form at the edges. Add the chocolate morsels and remove the pan from the heat, stirring until the chocolate melts. Add the 1½ tablespoons of butter and continue to stir until smooth. Let cool for three minutes. Transfer the chocolate to a large deep glass bowl. Dip the top of each cupcake into the chocolate to coat, letting the excess chocolate drip back into the bowl. Let the cupcakes rest on a wire rack set over newspapers until the chocolate is set, about 30 minutes.

7 Make the frosting decoration: In a small bowl, beat the ¼ cup of butter and the ½ cup of powdered sugar together until smooth, about two minutes. Transfer the frosting to a piping bag and decorate the top of each cupcake with a curlicue pattern. Serve immediately. Store in an airtight container for up to 2 days.

SNO BALLS

HANDS-ON TIME
30 minutes

TOTAL TIME
1 hour,
30 minutes

For so many of us, Sno Balls were a bridge too far. The color of dish soap and slathered in sweetened coconut, these treats were simply way too much of everything we held dear—sugary, oversize, offensive to adults—and, in so being, a bit profane. I can remember only one kid ever bringing one to lunch, and she also ate erasers off the No. 2 pencils in the back of algebra class. Still, I felt compelled to grapple with the Sno Ball because of its importance to the overall junk food canon. Who among us has not been tempted to bite into its crusty pink outer layer to see what lay beneath its crust? (This reminds me of the drawings of earth that we were forced to make in fourth grade. I got an F for titling mine "Home Sweet Home," which I still feel very sad about.)

What we have done here is elevate the common Sno Ball into something between a donut and the precious cake pop—a soft confection doused in properly toasted coconut, releasing a hint of the tropics while teasing us with its slightly gooey marshmallow center. The greatest test audience was my own child's fourth grade class, an age group notoriously hostile to coconut, who yet devoured the cakes. No one knew that they were supposed to be pink (they were not), because of course they'd never seen the original!

Makes approximately 40 small cake bites

for the cake

½ cup (1 stick) salted butter
1 cup granulated sugar
1 large egg
½ cup cocoa powder
1¾ cups all-purpose flour
½ teaspoon baking soda
¼ teaspoon salt
¼ cup whole milk
40 mini marshmallows

for the topping

2½ cups sweetened coconut flakes

1 Preheat the oven to 325°F. Grease a donut hole pan (see Note) with unsalted butter.

2 Make the cake batter: In a heavy-duty stand mixer, cream the stick of butter and the granulated sugar together on medium speed just until light and fluffy, about 1 minute. Add the egg and mix just until combined. Stir the cocoa and ⅓ cup hot water together until smooth. With the mixer on low speed, add the cocoa mixture to the butter mixture, stirring for an additional 10 seconds.

3 In a separate bowl, whisk together the flour, baking soda, and salt. With the mixer on low speed, gradually add the flour mixture to the butter mixture in batches alternating with the milk, beginning and ending with the flour and beating after each addition until the ingredients are just blended.

RECIPE CONTINUES

for the frosting

1½ cups marshmallow fluff

¾ cup (1½ sticks) salted butter, softened

3 cups powdered sugar

NOTE: I use a donut hole cake pan in making these—it's inexpensive and is very fun to own. You can purchase one at many baking and cooking retailers online.

4 Scoop a heaping tablespoon of batter into each donut hole cavity. Place a marshmallow into the center of each scoop of batter and cover the marshmallow with batter, ensuring that each marshmallow is completely coated. The pan hole should be two-thirds full. Bake for 10 to 12 minutes, or until the cakes are set, Remove the pan from the oven, but keep the oven on to toast your coconut. Let the cakes cool in the pan on a wire rack for 10 minutes, then gently lift the cakes from the pan, placing them back on the wire rack to cool to room temperature.

5 Toast the coconut: Place the coconut flakes on a parchment-lined baking sheet and bake in the oven for about 10 minutes, or until the flakes starts to turn golden brown, but no darker.

6 Make the frosting: With a stand mixer or an electric hand mixer, beat the marshmallow fluff, the ¾ cup of butter, and the powdered sugar for 1 minute at medium speed until light and fluffy. Transfer the frosting to a piping bag.

7 Frost the cakes: Place the cooled cakes, spaced generously apart, on a wire rack set over a rimmed baking pan. Starting at the base of each cake, pipe a spiraling circle of frosting around the cake, ensuring that it is completely covered in frosting. (You can use your damp fingers to smooth frosting over any gaps.)

8 Use your paws to lightly pack each cake in toasted coconut so that each entire cake is covered completely in coconut. (Don't just roll the cakes, or the coconut won't quite stick.) Use the rimmed baking sheet to catch any coconut flakes that fall through the wire rack, which can be applied to any semi-naked cakes. Store in the refrigerator for up to 1 day.

FUNNY BONES

For many snack cake fans, Funny Bones were a sort of also-ran, the thing that would be acceptable to munch on only in the absence of Ring Dings or Twinkies. My friend Glenn, who used to clock many afterschool hours at the Te Amo cigar shop near the Avenue U subway station in Brooklyn, would buy up snacks to scarf on the D train home, and remembers the Funny Bones as being "sort of dusty, because no one liked them." But this sort of trash talk is not brooked by fans of Funny Bones, a peanut butter–filled confection that went a step beyond the pedestrian chocolate snack cake. This cake is really fun to make, and you can fill it easily with an infuser or a pastry bag or even a plastic freezer baggie packed tightly with your peanut butter filling. The key is freezing the cakes before you dip them in the chocolate glaze, which keeps the crumb on properly and lets the glaze really cling. *Makes approximately 24 snack cakes*

for the cake

1 cup (2 sticks) salted butter
2 cups granulated sugar
2 large eggs
1 cup cocoa powder
2½ cups all-purpose flour
1 teaspoon baking soda
¼ teaspoon salt
½ cup whole milk

for the filling

1 cup smooth peanut butter
½ cup (1 stick) salted butter, softened
½ cup powdered sugar
½ teaspoon salt

1 Preheat the oven to 350°F. Grease a muffin tin or canoe pan with unsalted butter.

2 Make the cake batter: In the bowl of a heavy-duty stand mixer, beat the 2 sticks of butter and the granulated sugar together on medium speed just until light and fluffy, about 1 minute. Add the eggs, one at a time, and mix just until combined. In a measuring cup, stir ⅔ cup of hot water and the cocoa together by hand until smooth. With the mixer on low speed, add the cocoa mixture to the butter mixture and mix for an additional 10 seconds.

3 In a separate bowl, whisk together the flour, baking soda, and salt. With the mixer on low speed, add the flour mixture to the butter mixture in batches alternating with the milk, beginning and ending with the flour and beating after each addition until the ingredients are just blended. Fill the muffin tin or canoe pan half full of batter.

4 Bake for 18 to 20 minutes, or until the cakes are set and a toothpick inserted in the middle comes out with just a few cake crumbs attached. Let the cakes cool in the pan for 10 minutes on a wire rack, then turn the cakes out onto a wire rack to finish cooling.

for the glaze

5 cups powdered sugar

1 cup half-and-half

2 cups (12 ounces) semisweet chocolate morsels

NOTE: When you make the glaze, be sure the chocolate is cool before adding the cream and sugar so there is no nasty fat separation.

5 Make the filling: Using an electric hand mixer or a heavy-duty stand mixer, beat the peanut butter, the ½ cup of butter, the ½ cup of powdered sugar, and the salt together for 2 minutes, or until well combined and fluffy. Transfer the filling to a piping bag.

6 Turn each cake on its side and make a small channel all the way through the middle of the cake using the handle-end of a spoon. With the cake still on its side, fill the cavity with the peanut butter filling, taking care to pipe just to the edge of the cakes. Place the cakes in the freezer on a baking sheet, if possible, or stack them gently in a container. This will help ease the glazing process; 30 minutes should be ample time.

7 Make the glaze: Whisk together the 5 cups of powdered sugar and the half-and-half until smooth in a medium-size bowl. In a microwave-safe bowl, microwave the chocolate morsels for 1 minute, or until smooth, stirring after 30 seconds (see Note). By hand, stir the melted chocolate into the glaze until smooth. Holding the cakes upside down, dip them into the chocolate glaze, letting the excess glaze run back into the bowl, turning as necessary to cover all sides.

8 As each cake is finished, turn it right side up on a wire rack. Allow the cakes to set completely, about 1 hour. Store in an airtight container for up to 3 days.

FRUITY TREATS AND FILLED THINGS

My parents were hardly sticklers when it came to breakfast foods, but they drew the line at Pop-Tarts. When I asked my mother recently why this was, she said, "They were gross." When I pointed out that I used to eat a mixing bowl of Apple Jacks every Saturday morning while she and Dad slept in, she offered, "I was inconsistent."

I suspect that withholding moms understood that these breakfast pastries were essentially mini-pies. Of course, fruit turnovers were part of the dessert rotation in the early nineteenth century, as an extension of the meat-filled varieties made for centuries. But when Kellogg's Pop-Tarts were unleashed on Americans in 1964, they quickly became a cult hit, eaten warm at breakfast or packed cold into school lunches in that weird foil seal. The first flavors were blueberry, strawberry, apple-currant, and brown sugar–cinnamon; contemporary flavor bastardization has not left this treat untouched, and such abominations as Red Velvet and S'mores Pop-Tarts can now be found in some stores.

In an adjacent category of fruit-filled snacks is the fry pie, a southern staple to this day that was commercialized for mass-market consumption by McDonald's. As the legend goes, McDonald's founder Ray Kroc needed a dessert to sell with his burgers, and Litton Cochran, who opened the first Tennessee McDonald's in 1960, added fried apple pies reminiscent of those his mother made for him as a boy. The pies were a hit, and by 1970 the apple pies of Knoxville had made their way into McDonald's restaurants across America.

As a kid, I never quite understood apple pie eaters; their fruit choice seemed both pedestrian and bland, and I vastly preferred the cherry version. Sour cherries during a Michigan winter seemed exotic, and my best friend and I made a sport of counting the number of cherries in each pie—the record low was two, the high seven. Biting into those pies, fresh from the fryer, the sting of the fruit filling running down your chin, was a cheap thrill when you didn't have enough for a burger. Only when I became an adult traveling in the South did I appreciate the true pleasures of the proper fry pie, usually peach. Southerners also have the monopoly on mini-pies sold at gas stations; sometimes pecan, other times fruit filled, and occasionally chocolate, these treats are truly the great individual dessert.

Controversially, I usually consider Fig Newtons a treat, though one friend sniffed that "they are a hybrid dessert–healthy snack, one step above raisins." I feel this is a deep disparagement of this very fine treat, which is named after Newton, a suburb of Boston, and has the distinction of being almost completely unchanged since its arrival in the late 1800s. Its texture, as you will learn, is not easily emulated, but the perfect fruit-filled treat, like love, is a thing worth fighting for.

FIG NEWTONS

HANDS-ON TIME
1 hour

TOTAL TIME
2 hours,
30 minutes

When I was a child, Fig Newtons were the treat of last resort, the snack you grabbed when the Oreos were long gone, the chocolate wafers had been reduced to crumbs, and Dad had eaten all the windmill cookies. Soft, vaguely healthy, and not at all sweet, a Fig Newton seemed something best matched with a slug of Maalox and reruns of *Fantasy Island*. But my husband has always seen things differently. To him a Fig Newton is a soft, pleasant affair, a little bit cake-like, a tiny bit sweet, and full of exciting little crunchy bits.

I'm warning you up front now, so don't go sending me mean e-mails—this dough is extremely sticky (because of the high fat content) and hard to work with. Be patient. Be strong. The first time I made these, it was something like an episode of *I Love Lucy* as the dough stuck to my fingers while I tried to mold each cookie individually before baking. No go, babies! The next time, instead of chilling the dough in the fridge in one lump, I divided it into two pieces, rolled each piece between two pieces of parchment paper, and placed them in the freezer. You're essentially making a giant Fig Newton sandwich, and cutting it into cookies after baking.
Makes approximately 60 cookies

for the dough

1 cup (2 sticks) salted
   butter, softened
¾ cup granulated sugar
¾ cup (packed) light
   brown sugar
2 large eggs
3½ cups all-purpose flour
½ teaspoon baking
   powder
½ teaspoon salt
⅓ cup whole milk

for the filling

1½ cups dried figs
1 tablespoons plus
   1 teaspoon honey

1 Make the cookie dough: In the bowl of a heavy-duty stand mixer, cream the butter and both sugars together on medium speed until light and fluffy, about 1 minute. Add the eggs, one at a time, and mix just until each is combined.

2 In a medium bowl, whisk together the flour, baking powder, and salt. With the mixer on low speed, add the flour mixture to the butter mixture in three batches until just combined. Divide the dough into two equal pieces, placing each on a sheet of plastic wrap. Shape each batch into a 1-inch disk, wrap each with the plastic wrap, and refrigerate for 30 minutes.

3 Remove both batches from the refrigerator, discard the plastic wrap, and place each between 2 pieces of parchment paper. Roll out to a thickness of ¼ inch. Freeze both slabs for 30 minutes.

RECIPE CONTINUES

4 Make the fig filling: In a food processor, process the figs with ¼ cup of hot water and the honey for 30 seconds, or until a paste forms. Set aside.

5 Preheat the oven to 350°F. Remove one sheet of cookie dough from the freezer and place parchment side down on a baking sheet. Spread the fig paste over the slab of dough, taking care not to get any too close to the edge of the dough. Top the fig-covered cookie slab with the remaining slab of dough, parchment side up.

6 Carefully peel away the parchment covering the top layer and gently press the edges of the slabs together to seal the entire length of both long sides. Use a pizza cutter or bench scraper to trim the dough into a rectangle and remove the excess scraps (you can use them to plug any holes that developed when you peeled off the paper).

7 Bake for 18 to 20 minutes, or until the dough is golden brown. Remove each slab on its paper to a wire rack to cool for 5 minutes. Cut the slabs into 1½-inch bars while still warm to keep them from crumbing. (A big, sharp bread knife works well here.) Peel any remaining parchment paper off both sides and transfer the bars to an airtight container to finish cooling. Store at room temperature for up to 3 days.

APPLE-CINNAMON FRY PIES

HANDS-ON TIME
30 minutes

TOTAL TIME
1 hour

Here is the classic fry pie, in one of its best flavors. You'll want to eat these while they're warm, and fortunately they stay so for quite a while in a covered container. You'll be surprised by how simple the pies are to make. The key is the premade crust, which makes the entire process fast and easy and helps to re-create the authentic texture, except our homemade crust is far more flaky than the original. The demerara sugar gives them a perfect little sugary crust, the same one you no doubt remember sinking your teeth into during an unauthorized off-campus lunch. *Makes 8 hand-pies*

1 tablespoon unsalted butter

2 medium Gala or Fuji apples, cored, peeled, and finely chopped

½ cup (packed) light brown sugar

1 tablespoon all-purpose flour

1 teaspoon cinnamon

1 teaspoon vanilla extract

1 (14-ounce) package refrigerated piecrust (there are usually two per package)

1 large egg, lightly beaten

Vegetable oil, for frying

Sanding or demerara sugar, for dusting

NOTE: Demerara sugar, found in most grocery stores, is a large-grain unrefined sugar with a hint of molasses and a lovely golden hue. You'll like it.

1 In a medium sauté pan, melt the butter over medium-high heat. Add the apples and cook for 5 minutes, or just until the apples begin to brown and soften. Reduce the heat to medium; add the brown sugar to the pan, and stir continuously until the sugar melts. Slowly whisk in the flour and continue to cook, stirring frequently, for 10 minutes, or until the mixture is thickened enough to coat the back of a spoon. Remove the pan from the heat and stir in the cinnamon and vanilla. Transfer the mixture to a glass bowl and let cool completely (approximately 30 minutes).

2 Gently unroll both piecrusts and, using a 4½-inch round biscuit cutter, cut out 4 circles from each crust, for 8 circles total. Divide the apple filling evenly among the rounds of dough (about 1 tablespoon for each), leaving a ½-inch border around the edges. Using your finger or a pastry brush, place a thin line of beaten egg around the entire edge of each circle, about ½ inch thick. Fold over each crust to form a half moon, and press the edges together firmly to seal. Use a fork to crimp them shut.

3 In a large uncovered Dutch oven, heat 1½ inches of vegetable oil on medium-high heat to 350°F, or until a drop of dough sizzles and floats on contact with the oil. Cook the pies, two at a time, for 10 seconds on each side, or until the pies are golden brown. Using a large slotted spoon, carefully remove the pies from the oil and place them on a wire rack set over paper towels to drain and cool. Sprinkle with the sanding or demerara sugar (see Note) while still hot. Let cool for 15 minutes. Serve immediately.

LEMON MINI-PIES

HANDS-ON TIME
20 minutes

TOTAL TIME
50 minutes

Sometimes you are a person who makes your own *pâte à choux*; sometimes you embrace the perfectly good commercial dough. On days when you need a quickie dessert, these little pies get the job done with a commercial dough, a perfect impersonation of the store-bought brand, elevated by fresh interior ingredients.

In the commercial versions of these pies, the crust can be insipid, and the filling infused with corn syrup. But as I recall, mini-pies and fry pies hit the spot on long-night hauls on the freeway, with lights flickering from a truck on the other side of the road, the Go-Go's or Travis Tritt playing on the radio, and miles to go before you sleep.

This lemon pie is the ultimate high-low dessert: Your curd is worthy of a great lemon bar, but you're putting it in this pie dough to great effect. I've also provided a pecan version for those of you who roll with nuts, and a chocolate version because I want you to love me. Roll your dough very thin so you can get a dozen pies; it may look too thin as you press it into the pan, but it expands as it bakes. Patch any tiny holes with dough scraps. Do not overbake, because that will be the death of these. *Makes 12 mini-pies*

1 (14-ounce) package refrigerated piecrust (there are usually two per package)

All-purpose flour, for rolling out the dough

3 large egg yolks

1 (14-ounce) can sweetened condensed milk

½ tablespoon freshly grated lemon zest

⅓ cup freshly squeezed lemon juice

1 teaspoon vanilla extract

¼ teaspoon salt

1 Preheat the oven to 350°F. Lightly grease the entire surface of a 12-cup muffin pan.

2 Place one piecrust on a lightly floured surface and roll out to a 12-inch circle. Using a 4-inch round biscuit cutter, cut the mini-piecrusts and gently press them into the bottom and up the sides of the muffin pan, crimping the dough so that it just overlaps the lip of the muffin cup because the crust will shrink some in baking.

3 To make the filling: In a medium bowl, mix together the egg yolks, condensed milk, lemon zest, lemon juice, vanilla, and salt with your mixer on a low speed. Spoon the mixture into the prepared crusts, filling each crust two-thirds full. Bake for 20 minutes, or until the filling is set and the crust is golden. Cool the pies in the pan for 15 minutes.

4 Remove the pies from the muffin pan by running an offset spatula or knife around the edges to lift the pies out. Allow to cool completely on a wire rack. Store in the refrigerator for up to 3 days.

RECIPE CONTINUES

FRUITY TREATS AND FILLED THINGS

for the filling

3 large egg yolks

1 cup dark corn syrup

3 tablespoons unsalted
butter, melted

1¾ cups pecans, chopped

½ cup sugar

½ teaspoon salt

for the filling

3 large egg yolks

1½ cups half-and-half

1⅓ cups (8 ounces)
semisweet chocolate
chips

½ cup sugar

½ teaspoon salt

PECAN MINI-PIES

1 Preheat the oven to 350°F. Lightly grease the entire surface of a 12-cup muffin pan.

2 Prepare the piecrust as in the original recipe.

3 Make the filling: In a medium bowl, thoroughly whisk the egg yolks, corn syrup, butter, pecans, sugar, and salt. Spoon the filling into the prepared crusts, filling each crust two-thirds full. Bake for 20 minutes, or until the filling is set and the crust is golden. Cool the pies in the pan for 15 minutes, then remove, cool on a wire rack, and store in the refrigerator for up to 2 days.

CHOCOLATE MINI-PIES

1 Preheat the oven to 300°F. Lightly grease the entire surface of a 12-cup muffin pan.

2 Prepare the piecrust as in the original recipe.

3 Make the filling: In a medium saucepan, combine the egg yolks, half-and-half, chocolate chips, sugar, and salt. Cook over medium heat, whisking constantly, until the chocolate melts and the sugar dissolves. Continue to cook, stirring frequently, for 6 to 8 minutes, or until the mixture begins to thicken just enough to coat the back of a spoon and bubbles appear. Do not let the mixture boil. Remove the pan from the heat and let cool for 5 minutes.

4 Transfer the filling into a large measuring cup, then pour it into the prepared crusts, filling each crust two-thirds full. Bake for 30 minutes, or until the crust is golden. Cool the pies in the pan for 15 minutes, then remove, cool on a wire rack, and store in the refrigerator for up to 2 days.

SOUR GRAPE FRUIT ROLL-UPS

HANDS-ON TIME
10 minutes

TOTAL TIME
6 hours,
10 minutes

In medieval times, Arabs and Persians would dry fruits in the hot sun and turn them into leathers for long journeys, as the natural sugars provided energy. However, the cooler climate of the United States called for additional heat, and so now we have dehydrators. My earliest fruit roll-up memory is from my friend Jennifer's mom, a health-food nut who would purchase basic fruit roll-ups in the local food co-op. Modern commercial versions are more corn syrup than fruit, but we reverse that here. *Makes 8 pieces*

4 cups red seedless
   grapes, washed
¼ cup light corn syrup
1 tablespoon lemon juice

NOTE: The oven dehydrating time in this recipe is long, but it's needed to fully cook the roll-ups and let them obtain the right texture. You'll therefore want to make these when you'll be around all day, unless you don't mind leaving a low oven on while you run an errand.

NOTE: Should you choose to roll up the leathers, you'll need to do so in large loops, or they'll crack a little.

1 Preheat the oven to 175°F. Line a rimmed 11 × 17-inch baking sheet with parchment paper, leaving a ½-inch overhang on all sides.

2 In a blender or food processor, puree the grapes, corn syrup, and lemon juice for 30 seconds until largely smooth (some small pieces are okay).

3 Pour the grape mixture into the center of the baking sheet and spread evenly with an offset spatula. Bake for 5½ to 6 hours, or until the mixture is completely set and only somewhat sticky to the touch, rotating the pan halfway through to ensure even baking.

4 Carefully transfer the parchment to a wire rack to cool for 20 minutes. Cut the roll-ups into 8 equal strips, cutting away any brittle edges. Store in an airtight container at room temperature for up to 2 days.

Variations
CHERRY FRUIT ROLL-UPS

Instead of grapes, substitute 3½ cups of fresh or frozen cherries, pitted and thawed if necessary. Skip the lemon juice.

STRAWBERRY-LIME FRUIT ROLL-UPS

Instead of grapes, substitute 3½ cups of fresh or frozen strawberries, hulled and thawed if necessary. Use 1 tablespoon of lime juice in place of the lemon juice.

STRAWBERRY POP-TARTS

HANDS-ON TIME
30 minutes

TOTAL TIME
2 hours

During my early childhood, I was on occasion dropped at a neighbor's house for some early-morning babysitting—an event I found particularly loathsome, as I disliked her kids. Yet a mitigating factor was the Pop-Tarts, made doubly sweet with their cloying jelly interior and their very shortbread-like exterior.

The cornstarch gives this recipe a deeply authentic taste but makes the dough challenging to work with. The dough has a high ratio of sugar to flour, making the dough very sandy. This dough is best worked with after it's allowed to come to room temperature so it won't fall apart under the rolling pin. I fill my strawberry ones with some nice homemade jam. After they have cooled completely, they can indeed go into the toaster. (Not the cinnamon ones, which would do better in the oven if you're so inclined.) *Makes 6 Pop-Tarts*

for the crust

2 cups all-purpose flour
¼ cup cornstarch
¼ teaspoon salt
3 tablespoons sugar
1 cup (2 sticks) cold unsalted butter, cut into small pieces
2 tablespoons sour cream

for the filling

½ cup strawberry jam or preserves
1 large egg, lightly beaten

NOTE: I have skipped the frosting that adorns modern versions of these because I find it, in a word, totally gross. I guess that's two words.

1 Make the crust: In a food processor, pulse the flour, cornstarch, salt, sugar, and butter together 10 to 12 times, or until the mixture resembles coarse crumbs and only pea-size or smaller pieces of butter remain.

2 Stir the sour cream and 2 tablespoons of ice water together, pour into the dough mixture in the food processor, and pulse another 4 times. Remove the dough from the bowl and shape it into a disk slightly less than 1 inch thick. Wrap the disk in plastic wrap and refrigerate for 1 hour, or up to 1 day. If refrigerating for more than 1 hour, let the dough rest at room temperature for at least 15 minutes before rolling it out.

3 Preheat the oven to 350°F. Line a baking sheet with parchment paper. Using a ruler, trace a 3 × 4-inch rectangle onto a piece of parchment paper or cardstock and cut it out with scissors.

4 Roll the dough out to a thickness of ⅛ inch, and use your template to cut out 12 rectangles, recombining and rerolling the dough as necessary.

5 For the filling: Place 6 rectangles of dough on the prepared baking sheet 2 inches apart. Divide the strawberry jam evenly among the

RECIPE CONTINUES

rectangles. Then, using a spoon or offset spatula, spread the jam evenly over each rectangle, leaving a ½-inch edge free of jam around the perimeter. Using your finger or a small pastry brush, run a line of the beaten egg around the jam-free perimeter of each strawberry-covered rectangle. Cover each rectangle with one of the plain rectangles and press the edges firmly together to seal. Use the tines of a fork to score the edges over the seal.

6 Bake the tarts for 23 to 25 minutes, or until the tarts are a light golden brown. Let cool completely on a wire rack (see Note). Store in an airtight container for up to 2 days.

Variation
CINNAMON POP-TARTS

1 Make the dough and cut out the rectangles as described in the original recipe.

2 Preheat the oven to 350°F and prepare a baking sheet.

3 Make the filling: Thoroughly mix the brown sugar and the 1 teaspoon of cinnamon together in a small bowl.

4 Top 6 of the rectangles with 2 heaping teaspoons of the cinnamon-sugar mixture, leaving a ½-inch edge around the perimeter free of the mixture. Run a line of the beaten egg around the entire filling-free perimeter. Cover each rectangle with one of the plain rectangles, and press the edges firmly together to seal. Use the tines of a fork to score the edges.

5 Bake the tarts for 23 to 25 minutes, or until the tarts are a light golden brown, and let them cool for 10 minutes on a wire rack.

6 Make the frosting: Whisk the ¼ teaspoon of cinnamon and the maple syrup, powdered sugar, and vanilla together in a small bowl and drizzle over the pastries.

for the filling
½ cup (packed) light brown sugar
1 teaspoon cinnamon
1 large egg, lightly beaten

for the frosting
¼ teaspoon cinnamon
1 tablespoon maple syrup
¼ cup powdered sugar
½ teaspoon vanilla extract

ORANGE FRUIT SNACKS

HANDS-ON TIME
30 minutes

TOTAL TIME
1 hour

I must confess that fruit snacks were not a huge staple of my childhood, but I realize that at some point in the 1980s, kids started eating them in their lunches instead of actual fruit. My nephew Dustin, in his twenties, remembers them well from his Texas upbringing: "I would eat and drink things that were intended to impersonate fruit. Welch's fruit snacks, of course." No generic brands for this suburbanite. Although now he generally eschews such snacks for more adult fare, their nostalgic comfort component lives on: Dustin and his wife took giant boxes with them as backup food when they went to work as missionaries in Africa.

Our homemade fruit snacks—which I am happy to report contain only pure sugar—are a blast to make. I highly recommend you concoct them with any child who is not one of mine, who have long grown weary of my kitchen. You don't really need a pastry bag: just cut off the corner of a disposable freezer bag, and you're on your way. I squeeze my own orange juice for the orange ones, and they are quite good. I'm not big on advocating ingredient brands, but if you don't want to make your own lemonade and limeade for the lemon and lime variations, the Simply Lemonade and Simply Limeade products worked well in these recipes, while other products I tested did not offer as nice a citrus kick. *Makes eight ⅓-cup servings*

2 cups high-quality orange juice (for a potent orange flavor) (see Note)
4 (0.25-ounce) packets unflavored gelatin
1 cup sugar
Cornstarch, for dusting the snacks

NOTE: Hey, adults: you can replace 1 cup of juice with vodka, gin, or tequila to make these a party treat of a different sort.

1 In a medium saucepan, bring the orange juice to a boil over medium-high heat. Turn the heat off. Remove pan.

2 In a medium bowl, whisk together by hand the gelatin and sugar and stir it into the hot orange juice until the sugar dissolves. Let stand 5 minutes.

3 Meanwhile, using a sifter or wire mesh sieve, dust two rimmed baking sheets generously with cornstarch.

4 Fill a large glass bowl half full of ice and add 1 cup of water. Nest a smaller glass bowl in the middle of the ice. Pour half of the orange juice mixture into the small glass bowl and stir continuously with a wooden spoon until the mixture is cool and begins to thicken, about 5 minutes.

RECIPE CONTINUES

NOTE: Do not try to pipe your gelatin mixture before it is fully gelled or you will have a gloppy mess. Promise.

5 Once the gelatin mixture is the consistency of pudding (see Note), transfer it to a piping bag. Cut the tip of the piping bag so that the opening is about ½ inch wide. (You don't really need a pastry bag: just cut off the corner of a plastic freezer baggie, and you're on your way.) Pipe ¾-inch-long pieces onto one of the prepared pans, spacing the pieces close, but not touching. Repeat with the remaining warm orange juice mixture. Shake cornstarch over the piped candies, then shake the tray to coat the candies evenly. Let the piped candies rest 30 minutes.

6 Transfer the candies to a colander and, working over a sink, shake the colander vigorously to remove the excess cornstarch. Store in an airtight container at room temperature for up to 3 days.

Variations

LEMON FRUIT SNACKS

Replace the orange juice with 2 cups of lemonade. When you add the gelatin and sugar, add an additional ¼ cup of lemon juice.

LIME FRUIT SNACKS

Replace the orange juice with 2 cups of limeade. When you add the gelatin and sugar, add an additional ¼ cup of lime juice.

PINWHEELS

HANDS-ON TIME
15 minutes

TOTAL TIME
45 minutes

The sticky deliciousness of a hot cinnamon-laced bun can be sensed from a block away—all the way down at Things Remembered, where you were getting a bookmark engraved before you were lured away by a mall version of the cinnamon roll that has showed up in almost every American family. Great aunts make them, moms present them on Christmas morning, and every junk food company has its own version. Our pinwheels are made by carefully rolling out commercial dough; slathering it with your own homemade cinnamon, brown sugar, and pecan mixture; rolling it up and slicing it; then popping the slices into a muffin tin. If it looks less than perfect, this should be of no concern to you, because you will be lulled by the grandmotherliness of it all. *Makes 12 pinwheels*

¾ cup (packed) dark
   brown sugar
½ cup pecans
¼ teaspoon salt
1 teaspoon vanilla extract
½ teaspoon cinnamon
Butter, for the pan
1 (8-ounce) package uncut
   Pillsbury crescent roll
   dough
1 large egg
1 tablespoon molasses

1 In a food processor, pulse the brown sugar, pecans, salt, vanilla, and cinnamon together until the pecans are finely chopped, about 25 times. Set aside.

2 Place a 16 × 12-inch piece of parchment paper on top of a work surface and carefully unroll the crescent dough on top of it, with the wide end facing you. Evenly spread the pecan mixture over the entire surface of the dough. Starting with the end closest to you, roll the dough away from you until you have a 12-inch-long log. Lift the parchment paper to transfer the roll on its paper to a baking sheet, and freeze for 20 minutes.

3 Preheat the oven to 350°F. Grease a muffin tin with butter.

4 Remove the roll from the freezer, cut it into 1-inch-wide pieces, and place each on its side in the muffin tin.

5 In a small bowl, mix the egg and molasses together and brush over the top and sides of each pinwheel.

6 Bake for 14 to 16 minutes, or until the rolls are a deep golden brown. Let cool in the pan for 15 minutes on a wire rack. Gently remove the pinwheels from the muffin tin with a fork. Serve warm or at room temperature. Store in an airtight container for up to 2 days.

Chapter 5

SAVORY SNACKS

Soft Pretzels (VARIATION: Cinnamon-Sugar Pretzels with Cream Cheese Dip) ‖ Potato Chips ‖ Ritz Crackers ‖ Pizza Pockets ‖ Cheez-Its ‖ Chicken in a Biskit ‖ Fritos ‖ Funyuns ‖ Cheetos

For much of the nineteenth century, the thinking among medical professionals and most middle- and upper-class Americans was that eating between meals was unhealthy and déclassé, making one ill at worst and spoiling one's dinner at best, explains Andrew F. Smith, the respected food historian. Snack foods were largely relegated to special events. Pre-Prohibition, saloons sold salty snacks—just as bars do today—to encourage drinking, which allowed popcorn and pretzels to make early debuts in American life. (Street vendors, too, got their start with these foods.)

Even as commercial potato chips made their way onto the scene, distribution was highly local, as manufacturers were limited by a lack of packaging options. Wax paper was the encasement of choice, often ironed closed. There was no real sense of trademark or branding, and some foods were known only in a single town, notably Fritos, introduced in San Antonio in the early 1930s. As commercial potato chips and other salty snack foods began to take off, Lay's was the first company to take its product from local to regional to national.

Savory snacks were a diet staple during my high school years in the 1980s, and every new marketplace addition was as eagerly anticipated by my cohorts as Apple products are by my teenage daughter and her friends today. Too few people speak of Combos these days, and this hurts me deeply. And there were certain social codes transmitted through a Doritos flavor choice—Cool Ranch was beloved by cheerleaders, while the original Nacho Cheese variety was preferred by the hockey players.

But the classics, of course, endured. A ruffled potato chip was really for special occasions, like a basement party with sour cream dip. Otherwise, the thin classics would do. Pringles could be procured from a vending machine at the tennis club. People in the South seemed to adore pork rinds; in the Midwest, we were more interested in Cheetos, though they colored your fingers terribly, and you were often forced to choose between wiping your hands along your acid-washed jeans or showing up to driver's ed class with them dusted with orange. One friend, after a long bout of stomach flu, craved only cone-shaped Bugles. And for those of us tethered to latchkeys, a Pizza Pocket heated in a 7-Eleven microwave and followed by a Hostess fruit pie dessert made a workable dinner.

The fact that so many of these snacks still exist shows the enduring appeal of the salt-and-fat combination, and the pleasures associated with it. Football games, movies, and nights out at the bar are enhanced by their respective snacks, and in this era of baseball stadium sushi,

SOFT PRETZELS

HANDS-ON TIME
15 minutes

TOTAL TIME
1 hour,
30 minutes

No trip to the mall can be complete without a doughy, oily, slightly sweet pretzel, often paired with some horrible drink masquerading as lemonade. My teenager cannot leave the mall without an Auntie Annie's pretzel any more than she would consider departing without a few shirts that seem chosen to provoke me.

Pretzels have a long and storied history in American snack culture and were one of the original street foods sold in New York, first racked up on a stick and sold by women, later by men with carts. I was fascinated to learn from an exhibition at the New York Public Library that during Prohibition, street pretzels were associated with drinking, and thus ill repute, and were a snack food eschewed by the upper class. Later, the whole country learned to embrace their soft, tangy, supersalty goodness.

You can replicate this snack easily at home with pizza dough, either homemade or store-bought. (I recommend Whole Foods or Trader Joe's dough.) The real key here is a proper stretch to your dough. If you've mastered the art of home pizza making, you probably have this down, but if not, you will find this exercise a bit like putting pants on a cat. What you need to do is let the dough rest when it appears it wants to shrink. Roll it out as much as you can without breaking it, cover it with a damp towel, let it rest for 5 minutes, then try again. If there's no change after 5 minutes, leave it longer. *Makes 8 pretzels*

1 package prepared pizza
    dough (found in your
    grocery's cold section)
Vegetable oil, for the
    dough
1 large egg
⅓ cup baking soda
Kosher salt, for salting the
    boiled pretzels before
    baking

NOTE: When it comes time to salt, be careful to do so evenly, and do not have too heavy a hand.

1 Unwrap the dough and knead for 1 minute, either by hand or in a heavy-duty stand mixer using the bread hook attachment. Place the dough in a large glass or metal bowl that has been coated in vegetable oil, then turn the dough once in the bowl to coat all sides with oil. Cover the bowl tightly with plastic wrap and place in a warm, dry place, about 85° to 90°F, for 1 hour.

2 Preheat the oven to 450°F. Line a baking sheet with parchment paper.

3 In a small bowl, whisk the egg with 1 tablespoon of water and set aside.

RECIPE CONTINUES

for the seasoning

¼ cup granulated sugar
½ teaspoon cinnamon

for the cream cheese dip

8 ounces softened cream cheese
2 tablespoons powdered sugar
1 tablespoon whole milk

4 Fill a large Dutch oven half full with water, add the baking soda, and bring to a boil.

5 Turn the dough out onto a work surface lightly coated with vegetable oil and cut into 8 equal pieces. Using your hands, roll each piece into an 18-inch rope. One at a time, make each rope into a U shape, then cross the ends once and fold them under into the shape of a pretzel. Place the pretzels 3 inches apart on the prepared baking sheet.

6 Transfer the pretzels to the boiling water two at a time and cook for approximately 20 to 30 seconds each, flipping them after 10 seconds. Remove the pretzels from the water with a large, flat slotted spatula so the water can drain, and place on a wire rack to drain. Once all the pretzels have been boiled and drained, transfer them back to the baking sheet. Brush each pretzel with the egg-and-water mixture and sprinkle generously with kosher salt (see Note).

7 Return the pretzels to the oven and bake for 10 to 13 minutes, until golden brown. Let cool on the rack for 15 minutes. Serve warm or at room temperature with your choice of mustards.

CINNAMON-SUGAR PRETZELS WITH CREAM CHEESE DIP

1 Prepare the pretzels as in the basic recipe on page 118, through brushing them with the egg-and-water mixture.

2 Make the seasoning: In a small bowl, combine the granulated sugar and the cinnamon. Then, just prior to baking, omit the kosher salt, and instead sprinkle the pretzels with the sugar-cinnamon mixture.

3 Return the pretzels to the oven and bake for 10 to 13 minutes until golden brown, then cool for 15 minutes.

4 Make the dip: While the pretzels are baking, combine the cream cheese, powdered sugar, and milk in a bowl and stir until smooth, adding additional milk if necessary. Serve the pretzels with the dip.

POTATO CHIPS

HANDS-ON TIME
20 minutes

TOTAL TIME
**1 hour,
30 minutes**

The often-told story behind potato chips, or "crisps" as the English call them, is that they resulted from pique. As the legend goes, George Crum, a cook working in upstate New York, was being bugged by a patron who did not care for the French fries he had been served. So Mr. Crum sliced some potatoes very thin, fried them, and salted the hell out of them. The guest apparently liked them, and a snack food beloved by just about any snack luncher was born. Potato chips have since been adorned with vinegar and barbecue flavors and perverted with baking, puffing, and general overthinking. But a classic potato chip, simple and fried in all its glory, remains a thing of pure salty wonder. These days we have baked chips, pita chips, chips made of rice cakes. But when I bite into a good old-fashioned Lay's, or those favored by my kids, Utz Salt & Vinegar, I am transported to the days when I could eat an entire bag and still look more or less beach-ready.

Makes about 30 chips

5 medium Russet potatoes
**5 tablespoons kosher salt,
plus more for seasoning**
1 quart vegetable oil

NOTE: Once they've cooled, you can also sprinkle the chips with vinegar or barbecue salt, available in spice stores.

1 Peel the potatoes and slice as thin as possible (this is best done with the slicing blade on your food processor, or with a mandoline slicer).

2 Place the potato slices into a large bowl of cold water. Drain and rinse, then refill the bowl with water, and add the salt. Let the potatoes soak in the salty water for at least 30 minutes. Drain, then rinse and drain again.

3 In a large uncovered Dutch oven, heat the oil over medium-high heat to 365°F, or until the oil begins to pop. Carefully place the potato slices in small batches into the oil. Once they start turning golden, remove with a sieve and drain on paper towels. Continue until all of the slices are fried (see Note). Season with salt. Store in an airtight container for up to 2 days.

TREAT YOURSELF

122

RITZ CRACKERS

HANDS-ON TIME
15 minutes

TOTAL TIME
40 minutes

Crackers have their loyalists, and my household is no exception. My older child loves a Triscuit, that faux-healthy delivery system for hunks of cheese. My younger daughter prefers Wheat Thins, which I have always viewed as the more cardboard-like cousin to the Triscuit. But everyone loves a Ritz, which pairs perfectly with peanut butter, jams, and cheeses and is also great eaten straight from the box, one after the other. When I was growing up, the Ritz was the sophisticated precursor to the water cracker for adult party snacks, signifying a classier occasion than one meriting a mere saltine.

It is possible to emulate the buttery, melt-in-the-mouth texture of the Ritz, but it does take attention to detail. First, poking the holes in the dough all the way through to the pan is essential, otherwise the crackers will puff up and resemble rice cakes. You want them salty, but do not oversalt. *Makes approximately 50 crackers*

2 cups all-purpose flour, plus more for rolling out the dough

¼ teaspoon baking powder

¼ teaspoon sugar

1 teaspoon salt

½ cup (1 stick) cold unsalted butter, cut into small pieces

½ cup whole cold milk

1 large egg, lightly beaten

Kosher salt, for seasoning

NOTE: You cannot reroll this dough (because of the egg wash), so cut the crackers as close together as you can—a small juice glass works well as the cutter.

1 Preheat the oven to 375°F. Line a baking sheet with parchment paper.

2 In a food processor, pulse the flour, baking powder, sugar, and salt together 3 to 5 times, until just combined. Add the butter and pulse 20 to 25 times, or until the mixture resembles coarse crumbs. With the food processor running, slowly add the milk, stopping as soon as all the milk is incorporated and the dough forms a wet ball. Place the dough on a clean, well-floured surface and knead for 5 seconds, or just until smooth; do not overwork the dough.

3 Roll the dough out to a very thin (roughly ¼-inch thick) 15-inch circle, lightly dusting the rolling pin and the top of the dough with flour as needed. Whisk the egg together with 1 tablespoon of water in a small bowl and brush over the top of the entire surface. Using a 2-inch round cutter, cut out the crackers close together (see Note) and place 2 inches apart on the prepared baking sheet. Use a fork to poke 4 sets of holes in the top of each cracker (push the tines all the way through the holes). Sprinkle the crackers lightly with kosher salt.

4 Bake for 18 to 20 minutes, or until light golden brown. Remove to a wire rack and let cool completely. Store in an airtight container for up to 3 days.

PIZZA POCKETS

The Sicilians have their calzones, but Americans came up with the Pizza Pockets, a meal in the hand, less messy than an actual slice of pizza. You can easily jazz it up by using fresh basil and by sautéing the garlic in olive oil. Roll out your dough just the way you would a pizza, letting it sit after your first rolling so it can contract, then pulling it out again, as you did with the pretzels (see page 118). If this rolling annoys you, get a strong person to do it. *Makes 12 snack-size pizza pockets*

2 packages prepared pizza dough (from your grocery's cold section)

All-purpose flour, for rolling out the dough

1 (6-ounce) can tomato paste with roasted garlic

1 (8-ounce) can tomato sauce (see Note)

1 cup shredded mozzarella cheese

½ cup pepperoni slices, finely chopped (optional)

1 teaspoon dried oregano

1 teaspoon dried basil (or 2 tablespoons finely chopped fresh basil)

¼ teaspoon freshly ground black pepper

1 large egg

NOTE: I like to make my own sauce for this, by taking plain tomato paste and adding some garlic, chopped thinly and sautéed in a small pan of olive oil.

1 Let the pizza dough rest, unwrapped, at room temperature for 1 hour.

2 Preheat the oven to 400°F. Line two baking sheets with parchment paper.

3 Divide each ball of dough into 6 equal pieces. Working on a lightly floured surface, roll each piece into a 6-inch circle. If the dough shrinks back when rolled out, let it rest for another 5 to 15 minutes. Place the rounds on the prepared baking sheets, 2 inches apart.

4 In a large bowl, stir the tomato paste together with the tomato sauce, shredded cheese, pepperoni (if using), oregano, basil, and black pepper. Whisk together the egg and 1 tablespoon of water to make an egg wash.

5 Place a small amount of the tomato mixture, about 3 tablespoons, in the middle of the right-hand side of each pizza dough round. Using a pastry brush or your finger, place a line of egg wash around the entire perimeter of each circle about ½ inch wide. Fold each circle over to form a half-moon, and press the edges firmly together to form a seal, thinning the dough at the edge. Fold the edges over to form a lip around the perimeter to reinforce the seal.

6 Brush the remainder of the egg wash over the top of each pizza pocket and bake for 15 to 18 minutes, or until they are a deep golden brown. Let cool for 20 minutes on wire racks. Serve warm. (Uneaten pizza pockets can be stored in the refrigerator for up to 2 days and reheated in the microwave or oven.)

CHEEZ-ITS

I directly associate this snack with tomato soup, the perfect pairing throughout junior high, when consumed post-soccer practice in front of reruns of *The Rockford Files.*

The dough for our recipe is prepared in a food processor because, as Gail the baker explains, "the sharp blade and its fast rotation cuts the cheese into tiny bits quickly, dispersing them through the dough to promote a flakier texture." If you spooned these out into little balls, people would think they were a high-end cocktail snack. Cut into squares, with a neatness level that will depend on how compulsive you are, they are a bagged lunch treat completely loyal to the original. The paprika is responsible for the tang; the better the cheese you use, the sharper and more elegant the taste, yet they will still remain distinctly Cheez-It-esque. *Makes approximately one hundred twenty 1-inch cheese crackers*

2½ cups all-purpose flour, plus more for rolling out the dough
¼ teaspoon baking powder
1½ teaspoons salt
1 teaspoon paprika
3 cups shredded sharp cheddar cheese
1 cup vegetable oil

1 In a food processor, pulse the flour, baking powder, salt, and paprika together 3 to 5 times, until just combined. Add the cheddar cheese and pulse 15 to 20 times, or until the cheese is finely chopped. With the motor running, slowly pour in the vegetable oil and continue to process just until all the oil is incorporated. Wrap the dough in plastic, shaping it into a disk. Freeze for 2 hours, or until the dough just gives when pressed but holds its shape when picked up.

2 Preheat the oven to 450°F. Line two baking sheets with parchment paper.

3 Unwrap the dough and divide in two equal pieces. Place half of the dough on a piece of parchment paper and shape into a rectangle with your hands. Lightly sprinkle the top of the dough with flour and roll out, keeping the rectangle shape, to a thickness of just under ¼ inch. Using a pizza cutter or metal bench scraper, cut the dough into 1-inch squares. Transfer the squares on the parchment to the prepared baking sheet and carefully separate them, spacing them evenly, about 1 inch apart. Repeat with the second batch of dough.

4 Bake the squares for 7 to 9 minutes, or until the crackers are golden and the edges are beginning to brown. Cool completely on wire racks. Store in an airtight container for up to 3 days.

CHICKEN IN A BISKIT

HANDS-ON TIME
15 minutes

TOTAL TIME
35 minutes

This product violates my lifelong observed rule of dismissing all words that misuse the letter *K*. But my heart is soft for these crackers, which were fed to me by the mother of Chris, my high school boyfriend, as we sat in his basement watching the Bears lose. Those who grew up with this treat love its salty greatness and its sort of culinary baseness. As my colleague Carl said, "These crackers would be right at home in a lunch box on a construction site." Indeed. *Makes 50 to 55 crackers*

1½ cups all-purpose flour, plus more for rolling out the dough

¼ teaspoon baking powder

½ teaspoon onion powder

¼ cup (½ stick) cold unsalted butter, cut into small pieces

2 tablespoons chicken stock concentrate, such as Better Than Bouillon or Knorr (see Note)

⅓ cup buttermilk

1 large egg, lightly beaten

NOTE: Chicken stock concentrate is thicker and more flavorful than the stuff produced by powdered cubes—you can even jazz up your soup with it!

1 Preheat the oven to 350°F. Line a baking sheet with parchment paper.

2 In a food processor, pulse the flour, baking powder, and onion powder together a few times to combine. Add the butter and pulse until the mixture resembles coarse meal, about 20 to 25 times.

3 In a small microwave-safe bowl, microwave the chicken stock concentrate on high for 30 seconds, or until loosened. Slowly whisk the buttermilk into the chicken stock. With the food processor motor running, slowly pour the buttermilk mixture into the flour mixture, processing just until the mixture comes together into a ball. Whisk together the egg and 1 tablespoon of water and set aside.

4 Working with floured hands, remove the dough to a well-floured surface. Dust the top of the dough with flour and roll out to a thickness of about ⅛ inch. Trim the edges of the dough to straight lines using a pizza cutter or a really sharp knife. Cut the dough into 1-inch-wide strips, then cut each strip into 2-inch-long pieces. Use a fork to poke holes in each cracker. Brush the entire surface of each cracker with the egg wash before removing the individual crackers to the prepared baking sheet. (The crackers can be close to one another, but they should not touch, about an inch apart.)

5 Bake the crackers for 20 to 22 minutes, or until lightly golden. Remove to a wire rack and let them cool completely. Store in an airtight container for up to 2 days.

FRITOS

HANDS-ON TIME
15 minutes

TOTAL TIME
30 minutes

Fritos made their debut in the early 1930s, when C. E. Doolin, a San Antonio resident, became enamored with some fried tortilla chips he tasted in a café, likely the remnant of fresh tortillas used by Mexican cooks. He sold them out of the back of his car in little wax bags.

Fritos remain popular, in part because they are among the most unadulterated snack foods, really just some cornmeal and salt. They are divine at the bottom of a bowl of chili, or most properly in Frito pie, a staple of Little League fields in Texas and the Southwest, in which chili is poured into a bag of chips acting as a bowl. *Makes four to five ½-cup servings*

⅔ cup masa
⅓ cup yellow cornmeal
1 teaspoon kosher salt, plus more for seasoning
1 tablespoon vegetable oil, plus more for frying
¾ cup boiling water

NOTE: The first time I tried making these with cornmeal, they were a flop—the chips were soggy, flaccid, and weirdly salty. The key is to use masa—which can be purchased in large supermarkets and in any Latin American store— and to both bake and fry the chips.

1 Preheat the oven to 375°F.

2 In a medium heatproof bowl, whisk together the masa, cornmeal, the 1 teaspoon kosher salt, and the 1 tablespoon of vegetable oil. Slowly add ¾ cup of boiling water, ¼ cup at a time, stirring after each addition, until the batter is smooth. Let the batter sit until it is warm, but not too hot.

3 Place a piece of parchment paper on a clean work surface and pour the batter into the center of the paper. Cover with an additional sheet of parchment or wax paper. Roll the cornmeal dough out to a thickness of ⅛ inch. Remove the top sheet of parchment and use a pizza cutter to score (but not cut) the chips into small rectangles, about ¾ inch wide by 1½ inches long.

4 Transfer the chips and the parchment paper to a baking sheet, and bake for 12 to 14 minutes, or until the chips are set. Let the pan cool on a wire rack for 10 minutes, then carefully break chips apart.

5 In a large uncovered Dutch oven, heat 2 inches of vegetable oil over medium-high heat to 350°F, or until a chip sizzles and floats on contact with the oil. Working in three batches, fry the chips for 30 to 45 seconds until lightly golden. Carefully remove the chips with a wire mesh sieve to a paper towel–lined plate. Let cool completely. Season with kosher salt.

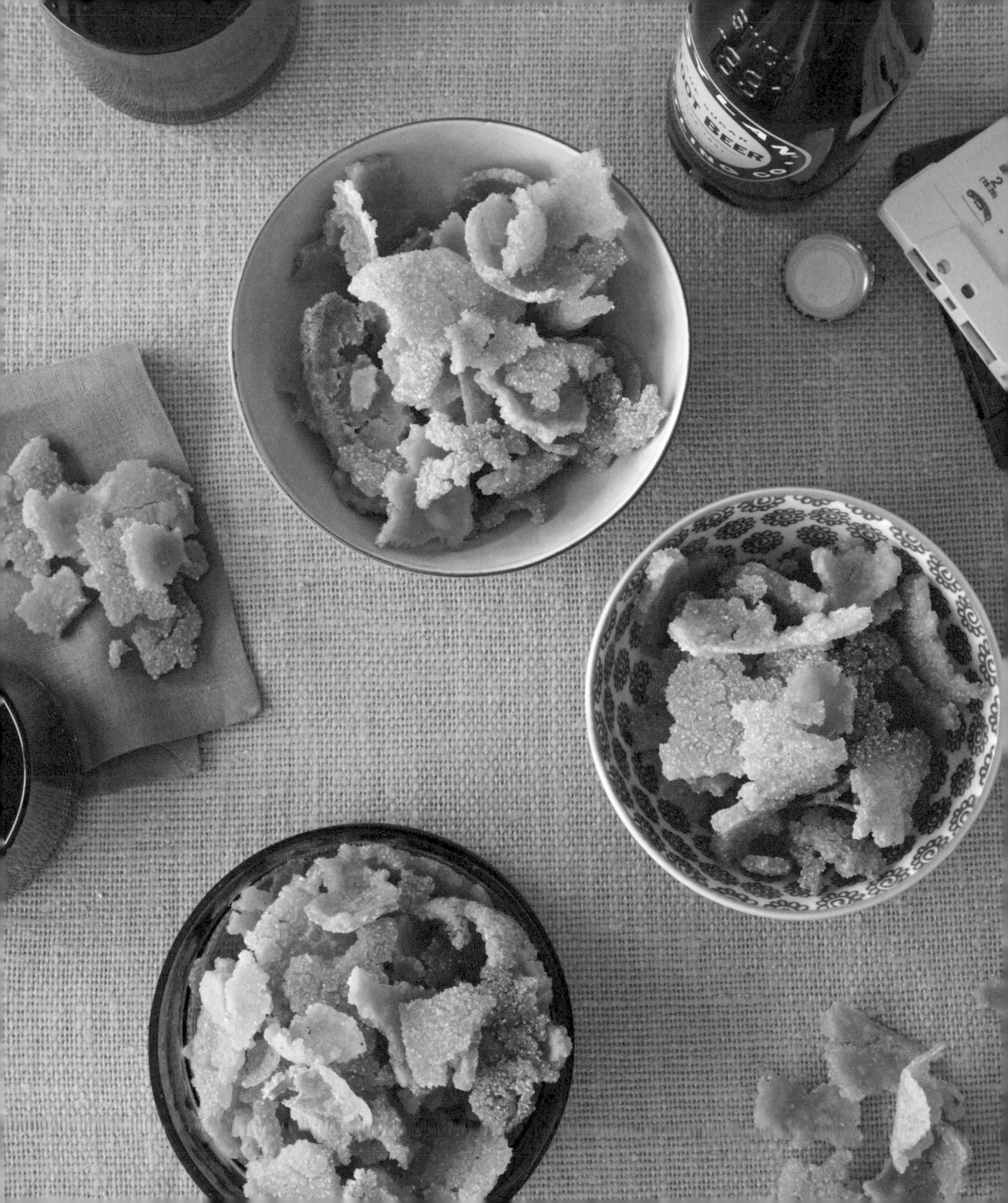

FUNYUNS

HANDS-ON TIME
10 minutes

TOTAL TIME
45 minutes

Funyuns are hardcore hangover food. A combination of *fun* and *onion*, they are also sort of ridiculous. There was something deliciously low-rent about them; my friend Roland well remembers hanging out on street corners in South Florida drinking Kool-Aid with his Funyuns, tossed back with a pack or two of Now and Later candy.

Our Funyuns are a great treat for a Super Bowl party, but they need to be served warm or they're just sort of un-fun-yun. The process for this recipe began with some onion-flavored panko breading; we then moved on to cornmeal, because it's more consistent with the actual Funyun. Pressing a thin layer of batter on a baking sheet worked best, a riff on an Italian-style polenta recipe. *Makes approximately eight ½-cup servings*

1 cup yellow cornmeal

3 tablespoons onion powder

1 tablespoon garlic powder

½ teaspoon freshly ground pepper

2 tablespoons salt

Vegetable oil, for frying

1 Preheat the oven to 300°F. Using cooking spray or butter, grease a 12 × 17-inch rimmed baking sheet.

2 In a small bowl, toss together the cornmeal, onion powder, garlic powder, pepper, and 1 tablespoon of the salt. Sprinkle the cornmeal mixture onto the baking sheet, gently shaking to evenly coat the bottom of the pan. Carefully pour 2 cups of water into one corner of the pan, to distribute over the cornmeal and lightly hydrate it while disturbing it as little as possible. Pour the water very slowly; if your pan is on a flat surface, it will distribute itself well enough.

3 Bake for 35 to 40 minutes, or until all the moisture is gone and the cornmeal just begins to darken. Let the baking sheet cool completely on a wire rack. When cooled, break apart the cornmeal mixture by hand into small, bite-size pieces of about 1 inch in diameter.

4 In a large uncovered Dutch oven, heat 3 inches of vegetable oil over medium-high heat to 350°F, or until a bit of cornmeal sizzles and floats on contact with the oil.

5 Working in batches, fry the cornmeal pieces for 25 to 30 seconds, or until light golden brown and crispy. Remove the chips from the oil with a large slotted spoon and transfer to a paper towel–lined plate to drain. Sprinkle with the remaining 1 tablespoon of salt. Serve immediately.

CHEETOS

HANDS-ON TIME
15 minutes

TOTAL TIME
2 hours

The Cheeto is never to be confused with its chip cousin, the Dorito. Though they are both unlike the potato chip, pure in intention and delivery of service. The Cheeto is all novelty, with its bright orange coating that covers the fingers, to be licked one by one as they emerge from the bag. One form is puffy, much like a cheese pillow, melting in the mouth; the other form crunches beneath the teeth, leaving a neon dust on your braces. For my pal Amy, the aroma of Cheetos is inextricably linked to the sound of canned laughter from 1960s TV sitcoms. My version is for the crunchy style but is in fact a bit less crunchy, due to the lack of preservatives, but deeply close in flavor. Its texture gets close, thanks to a low oven temperature at the end, and the dehydrated potato flakes, which are a great binder. *Makes 30 Cheetos*

for the dough

¼ cup (½ stick) chilled unsalted butter, cut into ½-inch cubes
¾ cup all-purpose flour
¼ cup yellow cornmeal
¼ cup potato flakes
1 cup (about 4 ounces) finely shredded cheddar cheese

for the cheese coating

2 tablespoons cheddar cheese powder (check your online food retailers if your local store doesn't carry it)
½ teaspoon buttermilk powder
½ teaspoon kosher salt
½ teaspoon potato starch

1 Make the dough: In bowl of a heavy-duty stand mixer, beat the butter at medium-low speed for 1 to 2 minutes, or until it is a smooth puree. Scrape down the sides of the bowl and add the flour, cornmeal, potato flakes, and shredded cheese. Stir together at low speed until a firm dough forms that can be shaped into a ball. Shape the dough into a disk and place on a large sheet of plastic wrap; wrap tightly and refrigerate for 1 hour.

2 Preheat the oven to 350°F. Line two baking sheets with parchment paper.

3 Pick off bits of the dough into tiny logs the size of, say, cigarettes, rolling them between your hands to form them into the Cheeto shape. Spread the bits out 1 inch apart on the prepared baking sheets.

4 Bake the Cheetos for 10 minutes, or until the pieces start to brown around the edges.

5 Turn the oven down to 250°F and bake another 15 minutes to crisp them up a bit. Transfer to a wire rack and let cool completely.

6 Make the cheese coating: In a large bowl, combine the cheese powder, buttermilk powder, salt, and potato starch. Add the cooled Cheetos and shake and turn the bowl until they are evenly coated in the cheese powder.

Chapter 6

CANDY

Marshmallows

Cracker Jacks

Fannie May
Mint Meltaways

Goo Goo Clusters

Twix Bars

Heath Bars

Candy Dots

Junior Mints

Raisinets

Payday

Mounds Joys

Like so many foods, candy was good for us before it was bad. Ancient cultures—and later Europeans—turned to sweets and candies for their perceived medicinal purposes, particularly those candies that were fashioned from fruits.

The foundation of so much modern candy is, of course, chocolate, which had value in pre-Columbian cultures in the form of cacao beans, sometimes used as currency. Christopher Columbus stumbled on cacao in the 1500s and borrowed it (or pillaged it, depending on your view) for his return to Europe, but it seems no one had much interest until the Spanish conquistador Don Hernán Cortés got wise to cacao's commercial value and helped spark its use in drinks. The dark underbelly of desire was in full evidence early on; candy production was at least partially responsible for the slave trade that evolved as part of colonization.

In America, boxed candy first came on the scene in the late 1800s, and incipient candy makers began to sniff out potential mass appeal. In 1900, the Hershey bar was released, initiating decades of development of the commercial candy industry, which was particularly heady in the 1920s, when Mars hit the scene and Fannie May Candies opened its first retail store. Candy also brought America its first real street food, the delightful Cracker Jacks, which were first sold in wax paper to keep them fresh, according to the food historian Andrew F. Smith. During the twentieth century, commercial candy extended its role as a health food to some extent, doled out as rations to soldiers (especially types with peanuts, such as the Payday) to provide them with big hits of calories.

Why not? We all self-medicate with candy. I remember when my oldest child, then about two and a half, fell down some stairs on Halloween. I comforted her with her first taste of chocolate and watched with fascination as misery untwisted from her face, which quickly became illuminated with joy. I knew how she felt. I used to hide under covers with a book and a Butterfinger after an unpleasant day at middle school, comfort myself with a pack of Mentos on long car rides, and turn to my beloved Heath bar on long walks home from work during my early days in Manhattan, when I couldn't afford to take the bus. While I now tend to keep high-end confections at my desk, like sea salt caramels and fancy candy bars, I'm not above the occasional midday Twix.

Making candy at home requires a bit of patience and is helped with a candy thermometer and some imagination. With the use of decent chocolate and other good ingredients, everywhere you sacrifice the authentic shape or texture of the original candy, you'll be exchanging it for quality.

MARSHMALLOWS

HANDS-ON TIME
20 minutes

TOTAL TIME
**2 hours,
20 minutes**

Did you know that marshmallow root is an actual thing? If you Google it, you will find that, prepared as a tea, it's recommended for many ailments. It was first formed into the candy we know today through a combination of marshmallow root, beaten egg white for lightness, sugar to make it tasty, and some sort of binding agent; we now use cornstarch and gelatin to serve that purpose.

The marshmallow tends to be the good shoes to go with a nice outfit: the accompaniment to hot chocolate or fudge, or the center of a fine chocolate cookie. Marshmallows are the basis of a few treats here, most notably the Mallomar. Making them at home is sort of fun, especially the part where you add the egg whites to your cooked gelatin and it all foams up like crazy in the pot. You do need a candy thermometer if you want to get this the right temperature and have it properly set. Remember that if you spread the mixture thickly, you will end up with big marshmallows (not that there's anything wrong with that).

Makes forty 1 × 1½-inch marshmallows

Unsalted butter, for greasing the pan and spatula

2 tablespoons cornstarch

2 tablespoons powdered sugar

3 large egg whites

1 cup granulated sugar

2 (0.25-ounce) packets unflavored gelatin

1 teaspoon vanilla extract

NOTE: You can make fatter marshmallows by using a 9 × 9-inch square pan.

1 Grease the bottom of a 9 × 13-inch pan (see Note) with unsalted butter.

2 In a small bowl, whisk together the cornstarch and powdered sugar. Sift half of the mixture over the bottom of the greased pan.

3 Place the egg whites in the bowl of a heavy-duty stand mixer fitted with the whisk attachment, but do not begin to beat them yet.

4 In a 3-quart saucepan over medium-high heat, combine the granulated sugar and ¾ cup of water. Bring to a boil and continue to cook until the mixture reaches 240°F on a candy thermometer. Meanwhile, stir the gelatin into ¼ cup of water and microwave for 20 seconds.

5 Once the sugar syrup has reached 240°F, remove the saucepan from the heat and stir in the gelatin mixture and vanilla. The mixture will quickly bubble and expand.

6 With the mixer on high speed, begin beating the egg whites to stiff peaks. Once stiff peaks have formed, adjust the speed to low and slowly pour the sugar-gelatin syrup into the beaten egg whites. Raise the speed to medium-high and beat the egg whites and syrup together until the mixture cools to room temperature, about 10 minutes.

7 Scrape the marshmallow base into the prepared pan and smooth with a lightly greased offset spatula. Using a sifter, dust the top of the base with the remaining half of the cornstarch and powdered sugar mixture. Let rest, uncovered, at room temperature until the base has set, about 2 hours. Slice with a pizza cutter or a knife into desired shapes and sizes. If you wish, you can line the pan with parchment and lift out the marshmallow slab prior to cutting, which will simplify the process. Once individual marshmallows are cut, they can be tossed in more powdered sugar–cornstarch mixture to keep them separated. Store in an airtight container at room temperature for up to 3 days.

CRACKER JACKS

HANDS-ON TIME
5 minutes
TOTAL TIME
25 minutes

Food historian Andrew F. Smith says this sticky treat was the first real street food. It traces its roots to Chicago, where in the late 1800s folks were selling popcorn as a savory snack from carts, and someone came up with the clever notion to add molasses, which was much cheaper than sugar at that time. Peanuts made the cut, too, perhaps under some vague notion that they were a protein hit. Suddenly, the candy world, which had largely been dominated by hard candy, often used as throat lozenges, was turned upside down with the idea of new forms of sweets, and Hershey's would come along with its goodies just a bit later.

Caramel corn is fairly easy to make at home, and it's great for a party—I first tried out this recipe on a group of teenagers for a sleepover, and it was a huge hit. You're making a big bowl of popcorn, so please make sure your kernels are fresh. Get someone with small hands and more time than you to unwrap the caramels (or you can make your own—see page 30). I made this recipe once with Trader Joe's sea salt caramels to give it an adult edge; it turned out great, though the little caramel packages took too long to open. *Makes 12 cups of caramel corn*

1 (14-ounce) package caramels (about 45 caramels)
¼ cup (½ stick) salted butter
½ teaspoon salt
2 teaspoons vanilla extract
12 cups plain popped popcorn
1½ cups dry-roasted peanuts

1 Preheat the oven to 300°F. Line two rimmed baking sheets with parchment paper.

2 In a large microwave-safe glass bowl, microwave the caramels and butter on high for 2 to 3 minutes, or until completely melted, stirring every 30 seconds. Stir in the salt and vanilla. Using a large rubber spatula, fold the popcorn and peanuts into the caramel mixture (see Note).

3 Spread the mixture evenly on the prepared baking sheets, and bake for about 10 minutes. Let cool completely on wire racks in the pan. Break the caramel corn apart by hand and store in an airtight container at room temperature for up to 1 day.

NOTE: Folding the popcorn and peanuts into the caramel mixture is mildly labor intensive, but you really want to do it with muscle, to make sure you get as much popcorn covered as possible. Be sure to let the caramel corn cool completely before attempting to break it into pieces, though it will be hard to keep your hands off the tray.

FANNIE MAY MINT MELTAWAYS

HANDS-ON TIME
30 minutes

TOTAL TIME
1 hour,
30 minutes

Growing up in southwestern Michigan, I spent a great deal of time in Chicago, which for us was the big city, rather than Detroit, which was farther away. An annual trip to Chicago—with Mom to go shopping and see a show, and later with the high school French club, ostensibly to look at French impressionist paintings before sneaking off to a restaurant where my fellow poor French speakers and I would attempt to order red wine—was the highlight of the year. And we would always go to Marshall Field's to get their famous Frango Mints, a truffle-like confection once made on the store premises. While those mints always had a special association for me, there are scores of similar products that have enticed generations of chocolate mint lovers, from After Eight Thin Mints, which the cool people's parents put out at the end of dinner parties, to Andes Mints, which my mother-in-law always kept on her counter at Christmastime, to Fannie May Mint Meltaways, a Valentine's Day favorite.

So let me just say I didn't feel all that enthusiastic when my colleague Carl ambled by my desk and proclaimed, after testing my first batch of Mint Meltaways, "Everyone agrees those mints are delicious and that they look like shit." The dough can indeed be messy to work with. The key to success is keeping your chocolate cold as you cut it; otherwise it begins to melt, and you have a white-hot mess. Also, use a very sharp knife and move quickly; if the chocolate starts to soften, put it in the fridge for a few minutes, then resume cutting.

Makes approximately 60 candies

1½ cups (9 ounces) semisweet chocolate morsels

½ cup (1 stick) salted butter, softened

1½ cups powdered sugar

½ teaspoon mint extract

12 (1-ounce) squares white chocolate

1 In a medium microwave-safe bowl, microwave the semisweet chocolate on high for 1 minute, stirring every 30 seconds, or until melted. Set aside for 5 minutes.

2 In the bowl of a heavy-duty stand mixer, cream the butter and powdered sugar for 1 minute on high speed, or until smooth. Add the melted chocolate and mix for an additional minute, or until smooth. Add the mint extract and continue to mix for 10 seconds. Divide the mixture into 2 equal pieces. Shape each into a rectangle approximately ½ inch thick, wrap individually in plastic wrap, and chill for 1 hour.

3 Line two baking sheets with parchment paper.

4 In a medium microwave-safe bowl, microwave half the white chocolate on high for 1 minute, or until melted, stirring every 30 seconds until smooth. Let the melted chocolate sit for 5 minutes.

5 Remove one chocolate disk from the refrigerator and let rest for a minute. Cut the disk into ¾-inch squares and drop into the white chocolate one square at a time, stirring gently to ensure all sides of each piece are evenly coated. Use a fork to transfer the coated chocolates to the prepared baking sheet. Let the white chocolate set completely at room temperature. Store the coated chocolates at room temperature in an airtight container for up to 5 days.

6 Repeat step 4 to melt the other half of the white chocolate.

7 Remove the second chocolate disk from the refrigerator and repeat step 5.

GOO GOO CLUSTERS

The innovative feature of the Goo Goo Cluster, invented in 1912, was its multiple elements. Packaged candies before Goo Goo Clusters were generally just chocolate. Mixing peanuts, caramel, and marshmallows with a lovely chocolate shell was a thing of wonder, right out of Nashville. The candies used to be hand-dipped and sold to order from drugstore candy counters; later, women would wrap them in tinfoil before machines were invented to do the modern automated wrapping.

Our recipe is a hipster rendition of the southern gas station classic—a rich, sinful glob of milk chocolate, marshmallow, caramel, and peanuts. You are less cooking than assembling. I suggest serving these on an elegant plate with a knife and fork. *Makes 8 candies*

HANDS-ON TIME
20 minutes

TOTAL TIME
2 hours

2 cups (12 ounces) milk chocolate morsels

8 chewy caramels, cut into 16 pieces

⅓ cup salted peanuts (the best are Trader Joe's blister peanuts)

½ cup marshmallow fluff, chilled

1 Preheat the oven to 200°F. Line a baking sheet with parchment paper.

2 Place eight mounds of the chocolate, about 2 tablespoons each, evenly spaced on the prepared baking sheet (you'll use about 1 cup total). Turn the oven off and place the baking sheet in the warm oven for 5 minutes. Using a knife or offset spatula, smooth each round of melted chocolate until basically flat. Top each round with two caramel halves, and evenly divide the peanuts across the top of each round. Cool on the baking sheet placed on a wire rack for 15 minutes, then refrigerate, still on the baking sheet, until chilled, about 30 minutes.

3 In a small microwave-safe bowl, microwave the remaining 1 cup of chocolate morsels on high for 30 seconds, or until melted, stirring halfway through. Remove the chilled chocolate rounds from the refrigerator and place a small scoop of marshmallow fluff, about 1 tablespoon, on top of each round. Gently dunk the top in the melted chocolate with your hands, assisted by a fork, and place the candy back on the sheet. Using a knife or offset spatula, smooth the chocolate so that all the marshmallow, peanuts, and caramel are completely coated. Let stand at room temperature until completely set. Store in the refrigerator for up to 3 days.

TWIX BARS

HANDS-ON TIME
25 minutes

TOTAL TIME
1 hour,
20 minutes

The Twix was my go-to candy bar, my movie companion, my lunchtime fascination, my trade-anything-for-it Halloween treat. When the mini-Twix came out, long after I became an adult who no longer had the metabolism to eat them daily, I thought them heaven sent, even though their arrival meant I would simply hide in my laundry room and mow down my kids' trick-or-treat bags' entire supply.

In the annals of classic junk food overreach, there was, for a short time in the late 1980s or early '90s, a moment of Cookies-n-Creme Twix bars, with a chocolate cookie base and an Oreo-like filling in place of the caramel, a devastating development. Thank goodness, the classic seems to have reigned.

This version is time consuming but worth it. Just make sure your pan is very well greased when you make your shortbread, or it will be hard to slip it out of the pan. Here's the good news: if the shortbread breaks, you can still set it easily into the caramel. But do NOT stack these once cooled, and especially don't stack them on top of your Goo Goo Clusters, or you will wake up in the morning with a glob of chocolate that you have to pull apart, perhaps in a dark room alone, where no one can see you eating approximately half a pound of chocolate for lunch.

Makes 12 candy bars

Unsalted butter, softened, for the pan

¼ cup (½ stick) salted butter, softened

¼ cup sugar

¾ cup all-purpose flour

¼ teaspoon salt

1¾ cups (10.5 ounces) semisweet chocolate morsels

1 (14-ounce) bag caramels (about 2 cups, or 50 caramels)

2 tablespoons half-and-half

1 Preheat the oven to 325°F. Grease a 9 × 5-inch loaf pan with unsalted butter. In a heavy-duty stand mixer, cream the butter and sugar on medium speed just until combined. In a separate bowl, whisk together the flour and salt. With the mixer on low speed, gradually add the flour mixture to the butter mixture in three batches, mixing just until all the dry ingredients are incorporated. The mixture should be crumbly but hold together when squeezed.

2 Press the dough evenly into the bottom of the loaf pan. Bake for 24 to 28 minutes, or until golden brown. Turn the oven off. Remove the loaf pan and let the cookie layer cool in the pan for 10 minutes. Turn out on a cutting board to continue to cool.

3 Wipe the loaf pan clean and line with a sheet of parchment paper, leaving a 2-inch overhang on each side. Sprinkle 1 cup of the chocolate morsels in the bottom of the pan and place it in the

RECIPE CONTINUES

still-warm oven for 5 minutes. Using an offset spatula, smooth the melted chocolate into an even layer. Freeze the chocolate layer in the pan for 5 minutes.

4 In a medium microwave-safe bowl, microwave half the caramels, about 25, with 1 tablespoon of the half-and-half for 1 minute, stirring every 30 seconds, or until melted and smooth.

5 Remove the chocolate from the freezer. Pour the caramel over the cold chocolate layer and top immediately with the cookie layer. Melt the remaining caramels and half-and-half, and spread another layer of caramel over the cookie layer. Return the pan to the freezer for 20 minutes, or until the caramel is set.

6 In a separate small microwave-safe bowl, melt the remaining ¾ cup of chocolate morsels on high heat for 1 minute, stirring every 30 seconds, or until melted and smooth. Let the melted chocolate sit for 5 minutes, then spread over the top caramel layer. (Do not worry about making the chocolate smooth, as the more you move the chocolate, the more it will mix in with the caramel.) Return the pan to the freezer to set, approximately 15 minutes.

7 Remove the candy from the pan by lifting the parchment paper lining straight up. Place the candy on a cutting board and, using a hot knife, slice the loaf into 12 equal pieces, each about ¾ inch wide, and peel the candy away from the paper. Let stand at room temperature for 10 minutes prior to serving. Store in the refrigerator for up to 3 days.

HEATH BARS

To me, the Heath bar was always the sophisticated lady's candy, the sort enjoyed by a teenager like me who preferred to sun herself on a silver reflecting blanket in the backyard, spraying copious amounts of Sun-In on her hair to turn it the color of tangerines. Let everyone else eat Hershey bars. I knew from toffee. I also loved how Heath bars were on the small side, hidden in an undersized package, discreet, almost sexy.

It took me a few attempts to get this just right, because I often would undercook the toffee, leaving a sticky mess, or overcook it to the point that it would resist even a pit bull's bite. There is a fine line between toothsome toffee and disaster, so you really need to stir it ten full minutes, but no more. Once the toffee is set, don't even try to cut it with a knife. Pick up the candy and break it up with your hands, or give it a mild whack on the baking sheet to break it up. *Makes approximately 45 pieces*

½ cup (1 stick) salted butter, quartered

¾ cup sugar

1 teaspoon honey

1 to 1½ cups (8 to 12 ounces) milk chocolate morsels

1 teaspoon shortening (optional)

NOTE: The best surface to pour your hot toffee on is a rimmed baking sheet, which makes it nice and thin so it won't threaten your molars.

1 Line a rimmed baking sheet with parchment paper.

2 In a 2-quart saucepan, melt the butter with the sugar and honey over medium heat until the mixture is smooth, stirring constantly. Continue to cook until the bubbles appear and the color begins to deepen. Stirring constantly, cook for another 10 minutes, or until the mixture is a light caramel color. Do not overcook, as the mixture will continue to cook and darken when removed from the heat. Pour the caramel on the prepared baking sheet and place it on a wire rack to cool completely, about 30 minutes.

3 In a small microwave-safe bowl, microwave the chocolate for 1½ minutes, stirring every 30 seconds, or until melted and smooth. If your chocolate is too thick, you may add the shortening to give it movement. Break the cooled toffee into rough 2-inch pieces. Drop the caramel pieces into the melted chocolate, one at a time, using a fork to turn them so that all sides are covered with chocolate. Use the fork to remove the candy from the chocolate, letting the excess chocolate drip back into the bowl, and place the candy on a piece of parchment paper to set completely, about 1 hour. Store in an airtight container for up to 2 days.

CANDY DOTS

HANDS-ON TIME
45 minutes

TOTAL TIME
2 hours,
45 minutes

Candy dots really taste like nothing at all, and yet they bring such enormous visceral pleasure. Perhaps because once swallowed, dots leave none of the resonant pleasure of chocolate or salt. The joy is largely in looking at them, and then that very first bite. Dots also served as kid commodities, exchangeable, scalable currency. My colleague Jonathan remembers dividing them in the open kid market; the boys wore them as bandoliers, while the girls stuffed them into purses.

These homemade dots are a great project for kids; just pop out a few on a piece of paper so you get the hang of it before blobbing up your actual candy rows. A pastry bag is useful, but not necessary. (I will save you the trouble: using a baby medicine dispenser will NOT work!) You can simply cut a tiny hole in the corner of a plastic freezer baggie, fill it with the candy frosting, and control the flow of frosting to paper by letting a drop drip out before you push any more onto the paper. Your thumb works as a great control device. Neon food coloring yields the most authentic result. *Makes 24 strips of candy dots*

2 cups powdered sugar
1 large egg white
Assorted tubes of gel food
     coloring

1 In the bowl of a heavy duty stand mixer fitted with the whisk attachment, Combine the powdered sugar, egg white, and 3 tablespoons of water. Beat on high speed for 5 minutes, or until the mixture is thick and glossy, almost holding stiff peaks. Divide the mixture evenly among 4 small bowls, about ¾ cup in each bowl. Tint each bowl a separate color as desired and transfer each batch to a piping bag or freezer bag.

2 Cut four sheets of freezer paper, each 5 inches wide and about a foot long. Using clear tape, tape each strip to a work surface with the nonshiny side of the freezer paper up. Snip small holes at the tip of each piping bag. Starting at the bottom of each sheet, pipe long rows of small dots, about the size of a pencil eraser, spacing the dots about ⅓ inch apart. Pipe rows of alternating colors in dots. Allow the candy to dry completely, about 2 hours.

3 Once the candies are dry, carefully remove the tape from the edges of the paper and cut each of the four sheets of freezer paper into six 3 × 5-inch pieces. Store in an airtight container for up to 5 days.

JUNIOR MINTS

On Halloween nights, my friends and I would always settle into someone's den to conduct an elaborate trading post with everyone gunning for everyone else's Hershey bars and Butterfingers. Mini Tootsie Rolls tended to be left on the pile with the tiny Bibles and random toothbrushes. Me, I tried to score the Junior Mints or Peppermint Patties.

This recipe is quite simple in terms of technique and ingredients, but you do need to pay attention to the temperature of everything. The first time I made the frosting, it sort of clumped everywhere. I added one tablespoon of shortening—I like Spectrum organic, which has no trans fats and is great to work with—and got the proper sheen I was looking for.

Makes approximately 120 candies

¾ cup (1½ sticks) salted butter, softened

1½ cups powdered sugar

2 tablespoons sweetened condensed milk

1 teaspoon peppermint extract

1 cup (6 ounces) semisweet chocolate morsels

1 tablespoon vegetable shortening (optional)

NOTE: The best way to mold these is to form the balls in your hands (flour your mitts if the dough is sticking to them) and then flatten them into mints. I tried making big ones and small ones and everything in between, and midsize mints seemed easiest to work with.

1 In the bowl of a heavy-duty stand mixer, cream 1 stick of the butter, the powdered sugar, and the condensed milk together on medium speed for 1 minute, or until smooth. Add ½ teaspoon of the peppermint extract and continue to mix for 10 seconds—the dough will have a pasty texture when finished. Transfer the mint dough to a sheet of plastic wrap, shape into a disk slightly less than ½ inch thick, wrap with plastic, and chill for 1 hour.

2 Remove the mint disk from the refrigerator and let rest at room temperature for 5 minutes.

3 In a medium microwave-safe bowl, microwave the chocolate and the remaining ½ stick of butter on high for 30 seconds, or until melted, stirring every 20 seconds until smooth. Stir the remaining ½ teaspoon of peppermint extract and the shortening (if using) into the melted chocolate. Let the chocolate rest for 3 to 5 minutes.

4 Cut the mint dough into ½-inch squares (see Note) and drop into the chocolate in batches of 5 to 7 mints at a time, stirring gently to ensure all sides of each piece are evenly coated. Remove the pieces individually with a fork and transfer them to a parchment-lined baking sheet to set. Let sit at room temperature until the chocolate sets completely. Refrigerate or store at room temperature in an airtight container for up to 5 days.

RAISINETS

HANDS-ON TIME
10 minutes

TOTAL TIME
**1 hour,
20 minutes**

The world is clear about Raisinets: they are for the movies, eaten perhaps with some Twizzlers, which have an off-label use as a straw. My friend Jennifer and I would wolf them down in the dirty-floored theater of Kalamazoo's West Main Mall, which had a fantastic mod fountain where we'd meet before the show, or at the old State Theatre while watching *Journey to the Center of the Earth*. Maybe once in a while Raisinets could be tolerated on Halloween, but that meant a tiny matchbox-size carton; the movie-size carton meant you could eat them by the fistful.

These little guys are trickier than you would think. The first time I made them, I simply dumped the raisins into the warm chocolate, and was left with a clunky sheet, like a chocolate raisin Venetian blind. Then I had one of those washing-my-hair-thinking-about-nothing revelations: what if I laid out the raisins, set apart, on a parchment-covered cookie sheet and drizzled the chocolate over them, then stuck the pan in the fridge to set? You have to use a fork to help coat the raisins, but the process works. Plus your raisins will be way better than the sad leftovers that the commercial brand seems to use. *Makes approximately 4 cups of candy*

2 cups (12 ounces) milk
    chocolate morsels
3 cups raisins

1 Preheat the oven to 200°F. Line a rimmed baking sheet with parchment paper.

2 Pour the chocolate into an oven-safe bowl. Turn the oven off, place the chocolate-filled bowl into the warm oven, and let sit for 10 minutes, stirring after 5 minutes.

3 Lay out the raisins on the prepared baking sheet, leaving room so they do not touch. Carefully drizzle the chocolate over the raisins, using a fork to help coat them by gently tossing them a bit. Let stand at room temperature until the chocolate is set. Store in an airtight container at room temperature for up to 3 days.

PAYDAY

Payday lovers are those who honor and treasure the pleasure of salt in their candy above all other ingredients. They are perhaps born, not made. My friend Steve distinctly remembers racing to the vending machines after baseball practices in Southern California. While the other boys zeroed in on Twix or Honey Buns, Steve was drawn to the Payday. Its salty peanuts magically replaced his sweat-out calories, while its caramel center spoke to his boyish sweet tooth. It's really no surprise that Steve grew up to be the man who prefers salted caramels to standard truffles.

A candy thermometer is really your friend here, because you can cook your caramel to the soft ball stage on the thermometer and know precisely when it is done. For the best result, cut the bars when warm. *Makes 8 candy bars*

HANDS-ON TIME
20 minutes
TOTAL TIME
1 hour, 15 minutes

1½ cups salted peanuts

½ cup (1 stick) salted butter

1 cup (packed) light brown sugar

½ cup heavy whipping cream

½ cup light corn syrup (see Note)

¼ cup smooth peanut butter

NOTE: Don't freak about the corn syrup—It Is not the high-fructose sort, but rather a member of the invert sugar group, meaning the sugar crystals that make it up are much smaller than those of regular sugar and keep the other sugar crystals at bay, so that candies like these remain smooth and chewy.

1 Line a lightly greased 9 × 3-inch loaf pan with parchment paper, leaving a 2-inch overhang on either side. Sprinkle ¾ cup of the peanuts across the bottom of the pan and set the pan aside.

2 In a 2-quart saucepan, melt the butter over medium heat. Add the brown sugar, cream, and corn syrup, and stir until smooth. Cook, stirring continuously, until a candy thermometer reads 235°F, about 10 minutes. Please watch for vigorous bubbling, and then keep watching the mixture carefully until the caramel starts to pull away from the pan and looks like golden spun sugar. When this occurs, remove the pan from the heat and stir in the peanut butter until the mixture is smooth. Pour the caramel into the prepared pan and top with the remaining ¾ cup of peanuts. Set the pan on a wire rack for 15 minutes.

3 Remove the candy from the pan by lifting the parchment paper lining straight up. Peel away the paper. Place the candy on a cutting board and cut into 8 equal pieces, each about 1 inch wide. Let the candy cool completely, about 30 minutes. Store in an airtight container for up to 3 days.

MOUNDS JOYS

HANDS-ON TIME
30 minutes
TOTAL TIME
1 hour

To paraphrase one of the greatest catchphrases ever in American candy advertising: Sometimes you indeed feel like a nut, sometimes you simply don't. The Almond Joy, of course, was for the nut lover, a coconut-and-almond confection smothered in milk chocolate, while the Mounds was simply coconut covered in a more sophisticated bathrobe of dark chocolate. What we do here is marry the best of the two: dark chocolate meets coconut meets a nicely toasted almond. The key here is to keep these babies cold, because they are not chemically stabilized and will not hold together super well sitting out all day waiting for your osprey-like colleagues to descend on them. But for an hour you're good. *Makes approximately 2 dozen small candies*

2 cups sweetened shredded coconut (packed)

1 cup powdered sugar

6 tablespoons coconut oil (generally sold as a solid in a glass jar)

1 teaspoon vanilla extract

Pinch of salt

24 whole almonds

3½ ounces dark or semisweet chocolate

2 tablespoons shortening or unsalted butter

1 Line a baking sheet with parchment paper.

2 In a medium bowl, combine the shredded coconut, powdered sugar, coconut oil, vanilla, and salt. (The oil starts solid but will melt down here.) The coconut mixture should hold together when squeezed into a ball in your hand.

3 Scoop the coconut mixture into tablespoon-size dollops and, using your hands, form them into rectangular blocks about 2 inches long. Place the candies on the baking sheet, and press an almond into the top of each. Refrigerate for 15 to 30 minutes, or until the coconut blocks have hardened.

4 In a medium microwave-safe bowl, microwave the chopped chocolate and shortening together for 15 seconds at a time, stirring between each interval, until the chocolate is smooth.

5 Using a fork, dip each candy into the melted chocolate. Let the excess run off each one, then, still using the fork, transfer the dipped candy to the baking sheet. When all are dipped, let set until the chocolate dries, roughly 1 minute. Refrigerate in an airtight container until ready to serve.

Chapter 7

FROZEN TREATS

In the pantheon of all things great, doesn't ice cream fall roughly somewhere between women's suffrage and the polio vaccine? I really wish we were able to celebrate the birthday of whoever brought this wonderful confection into all of our lives, but its origins are, like so much of food history, a matter of some dispute and mystery.

According to the International Dairy Foods Association, ice cream in some form was around as early as the second century CE, and Alexander the Great was really into eating snow flavored with honey and nectar (who isn't?). Biblical references suggest that King Solomon was fond of iced drinks during harvesting, and the IDFA notes that Caesar would send runners into the mountains to fetch snow to be flavored with fruits and juices. Many ice cream experts (no, not you—plowing through a pint of Chunky Monkey in front of *Downton Abbey* doesn't make you a scholar!) believe that Marco Polo found a recipe for sherbet in the Far East, which was later appropriated in Italy, but others believe the Chinese got there before anyone else.

The invention of ice cream on a stick is credited to Harry Burt, a candy maker from Youngstown, Ohio, who started with a candy lollipop in the 1920s that eventually morphed into an ice cream idea, mounting a chocolate-covered slab of ice cream on a wooden stick.

Several decades later, ice cream trucks became intrinsic to America's culinary culture. From the poorest neighborhoods to the snazziest suburbs, most children have grown up acquiring a Pavlovian response to the distant sound of "Pop Goes the Weasel" emanating from the end of their block.

Indeed, the arrival of ice cream truck treats defines summer. They provide the main food group of the community pool and, long before summer soccer camps and math workshops, are the central component of whiling away a hot afternoon, with nothing particular to do other than stare out toward the cul-de-sac, hoping for something to happen. Many ice cream truck staples are easily made at home, sometimes with just a few ingredients, including the all-important wooden stick, available at most craft stores. You can make them highbrow (with really good vanilla ice cream) or low.

These snacks, like the places and people they evoke, must be weighed in present time against memory. As an adult, the last bite of ice cream at the end of August may remind you of those syrup-splattered days you had as a kid, the ones that melted into back-to-school shopping. Or they might just make you lament the passing of time. But either way, they make you feel something, which is the point of all the treats of our youth, even when we believe we have left them behind.

CHERRY POPSICLES

HANDS-ON TIME
25 minutes

TOTAL TIME
**6 hours,
15 minutes**

Popsicles are the ultimate summer food, and everyone has their favorite color. My friend Jennifer's mother insisted that the purple ones gave her a rash. My husband remembers, with a hint of sadness, his parents making him share the duo-Popsicles with his sister, which forced a surgical procedure of snapping off one piece from the other, leaving colored ice crystals melting in the carpet.

Popsicles were presaged hundreds of years ago in various cultures where snow was treated with fruit juice, including the popularized Italian granita, which has been around, in some form, for centuries. The modern Popsicle was the brainchild of the early-twentieth-century inventor Frank Epperson, an amusement park lemonade vendor who once left a glass of lemonade with a spoon on a cold windowsill in New Jersey, the inadvertent first Popsicle. However, books and websites note that as far back as 1872, a couple of guys were selling frozen-fruit treats on a stick, a product they called the Hokey-Pokey, so who really knows?

What is clear is that Popsicles are great pool food. The juice trickles down your chin before you dive back into the water to wash away the sticky residue, one of summer's many distinct pleasures. *Makes 18 Popsicles*

1½ cups sugar
3 cups 100% cherry juice
(100% juice is less sweet and works better than concentrate, but use what you can find)

1 In a small saucepan, bring the sugar and 1 cup of water to a simmer over medium-high heat, stirring occasionally, just until the sugar dissolves. Remove the pan from the heat and let the syrup cool for 15 minutes.

2 Place 18 disposable 5-ounce drinking cups on a 9 × 13-inch lined baking sheet. To keep your Popsicle sticks in place when you insert them, put a piece of freezer tape across the top of each cup, pressing firmly to adhere the tape to the sides of the cup. Using the tip of a sharp knife, cut a small slit in the center of each piece of tape and insert a food-safe wooden craft stick through the slit.

3 Combine the cooled syrup, the cherry juice, and 4 cups of water in a large pitcher. Pour 4 ounces of juice mixture into each cup and place in the freezer for 6 hours, or until frozen. To serve, briefly hold the cups upside down under gently running warm water to release the Popsicles. Store in the freezer for up to 1 week.

GRAPE POPSICLES

While grape Popsicles are often relegated to the last-in-the-box status—like brown M&M's and black licorice, for no other reason than their being also-ran treats—I rather like them. Not as exciting perhaps as cherry, nor as avant-garde as lemon-lime, they are still sort of exciting and can be used to bribe small children to wash the car. Replace the 3 cups of cherry juice with 4 cups of 100% red or green grape juice. (Welch's is best.)

ICE CREAM SANDWICHES

HANDS-ON TIME
30 minutes

TOTAL TIME
3 hours,
45 minutes

The ice cream sandwich bridges that great gap between cake and ice cream, removing the choice for those who are torn between the two treats. It's the perfect blend of cookie and cream, like a frozen Oreo dipped into milk. My friend Esther remembers the particular ritual of eating one of these bad boys fresh off the cart, when you would peel back the paper and scrape off any excess with your teeth. From there you had to wait until the sandwich achieved the perfect state of "meltiness." If it was too hard, you felt as if you might break your front teeth on it; if it was too soft, you'd have a hard time peeling away the paper. Esther remembers sinking her teeth into the chocolaty "bread" as the ice cream center oozed out the side ever so slightly. Eaten just right, by the time you were done, a little bit of the cookie had rubbed off on your fingertips, giving you that last delectable lick.

The process of making these at home is not terribly difficult, but it does take a bit of time because you are basically baking cakes, letting them cool, then carefully spreading them with softened ice cream. *Makes 16 ice cream sandwiches*

for the filling
4 cups premium vanilla ice cream

for the cakes
1 cup (2 sticks) salted butter
2 cups (12 ounces) semisweet chocolate morsels
1 cup sugar
4 large eggs
½ cup all-purpose flour
¼ teaspoon salt
¼ teaspoon baking powder

1 Preheat the oven to 325°F. Line a 9 × 13-inch baking sheet with aluminum foil, leaving a 1-inch overhang on each side.

2 Prepare the filling: In the bowl of a heavy-duty stand mixer, beat the ice cream on medium speed for 1 minute, to soften and aerate it. Spread the ice cream evenly over the bottom of the pan and place in the freezer for at least 2 hours.

3 Make the cake batter: In a large glass microwave-safe bowl, microwave the butter and chocolate on high for 1½ minutes, stirring every 30 seconds, or until melted and smooth. Set aside.

4 In a heavy-duty stand mixer, beat the sugar and eggs on high speed for 5 minutes, or until thick and pale yellow. Transfer the egg mixture into a large bowl and gently fold in the melted chocolate, just until almost all the chocolate is incorporated. Sift the flour, salt, and baking powder over the top of the bowl and continue to gently fold, just until all the flour is incorporated.

RECIPE CONTINUES

5 Grease two disposable 9 × 13-inch baking pans, and line them with aluminum foil. Divide the batter evenly between the pans so each pan gets about 2½ cups of batter. Bake for 22 to 25 minutes, or until the cakes are just set.

6 Using the foil overhang, lift the cakes out of the pans and place them on wire racks, still on the foil. Cover the cakes with paper towels, allowing the paper towels to sit directly on the surface of the cakes. Let cool on the wire racks for 10 minutes, then freeze for 30 minutes still on the foil.

7 Place one of the cakes right side up on a cutting board. Carefully peel away the aluminum foil and spread the ice cream directly over the top of the cake. Top with the remaining cake, placing it upside down on top of the ice cream. Cut the layered cake into quarters, then slice each quarter into 4 equal rectangles. Place the sandwiches on a wax paper–lined baking sheet and freeze for 10 minutes. Serve immediately. Store in the freezer for up to 2 months.

PUDDING POPS

HANDS-ON TIME
20 minutes

TOTAL TIME
6 hours,
50 minutes

My father was no foodie, but he had two specific demands: in our house, there would be no American cheese (cheese food product is not cheese!), and any pudding must be made on the stovetop or it wasn't really pudding. Didn't the rest of the world know better about pudding? No, in fact, they didn't. Slow-cooked pudding has a deeper chocolaty flavor and often a more intense cream texture and is worth the extra few minutes, as Dad knew.

These pudding pops are based on the real stuff, chocolaty goodness thickened with cornstarch, then frozen into treats that would make Bill Cosby proud. In our recipe, plastic wrap laid on top of the pudding keeps it from getting that icky skin as it cools, although in truth, as a kid I always peeled off the skin and plastered it across my mouth, sucking it in and out like a small chocolate balloon. *Makes 12 pudding pops*

1 cup sugar

3 tablespoons all-purpose flour

½ cup cocoa powder

¼ teaspoon salt

3 cups low-fat milk

NOTE: As you cook your pudding, remember that you want it fairly thick before transferring it to the refrigerator. If it seems at all runny, keep cooking.

NOTE: Once you get the pudding into the cups, if you do not make an effort to smooth the tops, your pops will be sort of sad and misshapen once you peel away their cups. But they will still be delicious. Wax-lined Dixie cups work fine here.

1 In a 2-quart saucepan, combine the sugar, flour, cocoa, salt, and milk, whisking until smooth. Cook over medium heat, whisking frequently, until the mixture just begins to bubble and coats the back of a spoon (see Note), about 10 to 15 minutes, but do not let the mixture come to a boil. Remove the pan from the heat and let the mixture rest for 5 minutes. Transfer the pudding to a large glass bowl, cover with plastic wrap, placing the plastic directly against the surface of the pudding, and chill for 1 hour.

2 Divide the pudding among twelve 3-ounce disposable paper cups, filling each about two-thirds full (see Note). Place the pops in a rimmed baking dish and place in the freezer for 1 hour.

3 Remove the partially frozen pops from the freezer and insert a food-safe craft stick in the center of each. Return to the freezer for 5 hours, or until fully frozen. Tear the paper cup away from each pop before serving. Store in the freezer for up to 1 week.

ORANGE CREAMSICLES

HANDS-ON TIME
10 minutes

TOTAL TIME
3 hours,
10 minutes

The creamsicle is the less-high-maintenance cousin of the Push-Up—less watery, a tad creamier, and of course delivered on a stick, not through a cylinder. But the delivery method of the Push-Up is what triggers the craving: for many families, the Push-Up—made from sherbet and shoved into a paper cylinder—was the bridge between actual ice cream and a Popsicle, the former perhaps deemed too fattening, the latter too full of sugar. Eating Push-Ups in the sun was always an uphill affair, as their melt factor often exceeded the speed of one's tongue. But the joy of the creamsicle was both its perceived health value—I am not eating ice cream, I am eating frozen breakfast!—and its sublime feel in the mouth as the orange and cream came together in sort of a cloud of baby aspirin delight.

Indeed, part of the problem with commercial orange ice cream treats was that their orange flavor was inadequate, perhaps owing to the orange juice concentrate mix, which was never quite tart. But the creamsicles here deliver: I use fresh-squeezed OJ and really good vanilla ice cream—easy peasy. And I make eight large pops rather than many small ones—a deserved indulgence, they're so good. *Makes 18 Popsicles*

3¼ cups premium vanilla
   ice cream
3¼ cups premium orange
   juice

1 Lay out 18 disposable 5-ounce paper cups on a rimmed baking sheet. Allow the ice cream to sit at room temperature for 5 minutes to soften.

2 Using a small trigger-handled scoop or a large melon baller, scoop 3 rounded tablespoons of ice cream into each of the paper cups. Pour the orange juice over the ice cream, just enough to almost fill each cup. Then insert a food-safe craft stick into the center of each cup and place the pan in the freezer until the Popsicles are frozen through, about 3 hours. Tear the paper cup from each Popsicle before serving.

3 Store in the freezer for up to 1 week.

BOMB POPS

HANDS-ON TIME
10 minutes

TOTAL TIME
**6 hours,
10 minutes**

Red, white, and blue, distinctively grooved, and shaped like a rocket, Bomb Pops brought the Fourth of July to kids every day for the entire season and were a staple of the ice cream man. You chased him down in your neighborhood or thronged him at the community swimming pool, and on sweltering days, Bomb Pops had a distinct advantage over his ice cream products. They always seemed especially cold and melted much more slowly across a hot and likely mud-caked mouth. They also stained your tongue, a bonus for boys. You can also try various flavors of juice—including grape juice with blue food coloring for verisimilitude—to make a custom adult Bomb Pop to suit your fancy.

Makes 18 tri-flavored popsicles

3 cups cherry juice
    cocktail

3 cups limeade

10 drops blue food
    coloring (the gel variety
    available at baking
    stores is most intense;
    you may need more if
    you use commercial
    food coloring from the
    grocery store)

3 cups white grape juice

1 Place eighteen 5-ounce disposable drinking cups in a lined 9 × 13-inch baking sheet. To keep your Popsicle sticks in place when you insert them, put a piece of freezer tape across the top of each cup, pressing firmly to adhere the tape to the sides of the cup. Then, using the tip of a sharp knife, cut a small slit in the center of each piece of tape. Insert a food-safe wooden craft stick into each cup through the slit.

2 Fill the cups about one-third full with cherry juice, about 2 tablespoons of juice each. Freeze the cups for about 4 hours, or until the juice is frozen (this will depend on your freezer power).

3 Remove the pops from the freezer and pour the limeade into each cup on top of the frozen cherry juice, filling each cup about two-thirds full. Return the cups to the freezer for 2 to 4 additional hours, or until the limeade is frozen.

4 Mix your food coloring and white grape juice to achieve a blue color.

5 Repeat your freezing technique with the grape juice, pouring it nearly to the top over your already frozen juice. Freeze until the Popsicles are completely set, about 3 hours. To serve, briefly hold the cups upside down under gently running warm water to release the Popsicles. Store in the freezer for up to 1 week.

STRAWBERRY SHORTCAKE ICE CREAM POPS

HANDS-ON TIME
15 minutes

TOTAL TIME
3 hours,
25 minutes

There was always that one kid, the iconoclast among all of us tasting our first bit of autonomy, who went for the Strawberry Shortcake bars. My friend Andrea steered clear of them because they were her sister's thing. "Both the Chocolate Éclair and the Strawberry Shortcake bars were kind of the crème de la crème of the ice cream truck," Andrea recalled. She added: "I mostly think of them as the alternative to the chocolate version, and because they are intimately bound up in my childhood sense of choosing different things than my sister did, I also think of them as the Kerry doll to the Chrissy doll." *Makes 2½ cups of ice cream or six 4-ounce ice cream pops*

1 cup yellow cake crumbs (about 2 cupcakes or ¼ of a loaf pound cake)
1½ cups finely diced strawberries
1 pint premium vanilla ice cream

NOTE: Overmixing the ice cream will beat in too much air, which may mean faster melting, which will cause your mix to crystallize when frozen.

NOTE: If you don't have Popsicle molds, transfer the ice cream to a loaf pan and freeze until set. Serve scoops on ice cream cones.

1 Crumble the cake with your hands until you have evenly broken-apart but not too fine cake crumbs. Preheat the oven to 325°F. Line two rimmed baking sheets with parchment paper.

2 Spread the cake crumbs over one of the prepared baking sheets and bake for 10 to 13 minutes, or until golden brown. Remove to a wire rack to cool completely.

3 Spread the diced strawberries in a single layer on the second prepared baking sheet. Transfer the strawberry- and crumb-filled pans to the freezer and let freeze for 1 hour.

4 Remove the ice cream from the freezer and let it rest at room temperature for 5 minutes, until just soft enough to scoop, then transfer it to a heavy-duty stand mixer. Using the paddle attachment, beat the ice cream on medium speed for 15 seconds, or just until it starts to become smooth. Add the frozen cake and strawberry pieces and beat for just 10 seconds more. Do not overmix (see Note). Transfer the ice cream mixture to Popsicle molds (see Note) and freeze for 2 hours. Run the molds briefly under gently running warm water to loosen the pops. Store in the freezer for up to 2 months.

NUTTY BUDDIES

HANDS-ON TIME
15 minutes

TOTAL TIME
45 minutes

My friend Carl remembers that when he was a kid growing up in Ottawa, Illinois, back in the 1960s, "My favorite store was the Dairy Bar at the corner of State and Center Streets. It was the main neighborhood stop for ice cream and other confections like orange sherbet Push-Ups and Eskimo Pies. I liked those, but I always gravitated toward the Drumstick."

The only trick with this recipe is making sure you have enough room in your freezer to hold all the tall cups needed to hold up the cones and that the cups are deep enough. Of all the recipes for this book, Carl proclaimed these the most genuinely authentic to his memories. "The whole thing had the feeling of a real Nutty Buddy that you better eat up because it could fall off the cone at any time." I am happy to give him the last word. *Makes 12 dipped ice cream cones*

12 sugar cones
2 cups (12 ounces) semisweet chocolate morsels
¼ cup vegetable oil
8 cups premium vanilla ice cream
1 cup toasted pecans, chopped

1 Place the ice cream cones upright in 12 freezer-safe cups.

2 In a medium microwave-safe bowl, microwave the chocolate on high for 90 seconds, stirring every 30 seconds, or until melted. Stir the vegetable oil into the melted chocolate until smooth. Pour 1 teaspoon of the melted chocolate mixture into the bottom of each ice cream cone. (Reserve the rest in the bowl.) After the chocolate in the cones has cooled to room temperature, freeze the cones in their cups for 30 minutes.

3 Scoop ⅔ cup of ice cream into each cone, carefully packing the ice cream into the base of the cone and leaving a rounded top on each. Return the cones in their cups to the freezer for 30 minutes.

4 Working with one at a time, remove the cones from the freezer and spoon the remaining melted chocolate over the ice cream. If the chocolate has hardened, microwave for 30 seconds to warm. Hold the cones at an angle and turn to ensure that they are evenly coated, allowing the excess chocolate to drip back into the bowl. Move quickly, as the chocolate on the cone will harden almost instantly. Sprinkle the tops immediately with the chopped pecans. Return the cones to the freezer until ready to serve, setting them in cups to keep them upright. Store in the freezer for up to 1 day.

ACKNOWLEDGMENTS

This cookbook never could have come together without the enormous generosity and taste buds of my *New York Times* family, beginning with Susan Edgerley, who published my original article about making homemade junk food, and extending to the entire Washington bureau staff, who diligently plowed through failed candy bars, burned cookies, and substandard Twinkies, providing salient commentary, childhood memories, and encouragement over many, many months. Special thanks goes to Carl Hulse, who tasted every single recipe and never lied about one.

I am also indebted to my many friends, family, and colleagues who shared their junk food stories, especially Amy Albert, Frank Bruni, Esther Fein, Andrea Levine, Jennifer Farrington, Dustin Koctar, Mike Shear, Lynn Steinhauer, and Jonathan Weisman. Cathy Barrow and Gail Dosik provided invaluable technical expertise, as did the incomparable Emily Vann. Amanda Hesser, Merrill Stubbs, and their entire team at food52.com provided incalculable support and space to talk cupcakes. James Ransom brought his lovely eye to the photographs, aided by the talented Stephanie Hanes, our prop stylist, and Karen Evans, the best food stylist around.

For historic references, I am indebted to the food historians Andrew F. Smith and Lynne Olver and her indispensable foodtimeline.org, which aggregates food history. I referred also to several great resources on junk food, including *Sweet Tooth: The Bittersweet History of Candy*, by Kate Hopkins, and *The Great American Ice Cream Book*, by Paul Dickson, as well as the websites mybakingaddiction.com and joyofbaking.com.

I am intensely grateful to Alia Hanna Habib at McCormick & Williams, the agent who is the envy of all my writer friends, for acknowledging the joy of junk food, and the wonderful and talented Jessica Freeman-Slade, my editor at Clarkson Potter, for seeing it all through. Thanks to the entire Clarkson Potter team, including Patricia Shaw, Kim Tyner, Carly Gorga, Anna Mintz, Jane Treuhaft, Jim Massey, and Rae Ann Spitzenberger.

Last but never least, I must thank my wonderful husband, Edward Wyatt, who copyedited, commented, and tasted with patience and love. Now, we will diet.

INDEX